CONTENTS.

SIR FRANCIS DRAKE.

ROBERT BLAKE.

SIR FRANCIS DRAKE.

" *Drake, he's in his hammock till the great Armadas come*
  (Capten, art thou sleepin' there below?),
Slung atween the round shot, listenin' for the drum,
  An' dreamin' arl the time of Plymouth Hoe.
Call him on the deep sea, call him up the Sound,
  Call him when ye sail to meet the foe;
Where the old trade's plyin', and the old flag flyin',
  They shall find him ware an' wakin', as they found him
    long ago."—NEWBOLT.

Two Old Sea-Dogs.

SIR FRANCIS DRAKE.

CHAPTER I.

A Lad of Mettle.

WHEN Queen Elizabeth ascended the English throne, the country had been brought almost to the brink of ruin by foreign wars and religious strife. Now, Protestant and Catholic live amicably together, and we all enjoy freedom to worship God in our own way.

But in the sixteenth century, and for long afterwards, bitter enmity existed between the two great religious bodies; and, not in our country only, but throughout most of Europe, there raged a deadly strife between the Reformers and those who still held by the Pope. The Continent was a huge battlefield, and peaceful traders on the sea were compelled to arm in self-defence against hostile vessels. A terrible spirit crept into the hearts of men, who, gentle and forbearing in every other matter, became in the cause of religion, fierce, passionate, and vindictive.

Behind this difference in creeds lay another cause of turmoil—the struggle for mastery between the various European nations. Philip, King of Spain, was without doubt the strongest monarch of his time, and he used every atom of his power for the spreading of Roman Catholicism. Spain and Portugal were his; the finest portions of Italy belonged to him; Flanders and the Low Countries were subject to his rule. Far away over-sea his governors drained the New World of its wealth to fill his treasury; and every day his massive galleons were speeding homeward laden with the treasures of the West.

Nor must it be forgotten that no other nation could share in these spoils. The Spanish dominions were closed to all but Spaniards: the South Atlantic and the Pacific oceans were regarded as Spanish lakes, and an English sailor approached the coasts of Mexico or of South America only at his peril.

To us in these days it may seem strange that a king of Spain should have wielded such tremendous authority; but, as far as downright bravery and fearlessness went, the Spaniards were worthy of their high place. Their infantry were the finest in the world, and, though lacking the fiery dash of the French, were full of pluck, indomitable, and hard to beat. Their horsemen, too, were gallant and daring, ever ready to advance, ever reluctant to retreat; proud of their land, devoted to their religion, and resolved to make both supreme.

As on land, so on sea! Spanish sailors were

among the first to brave the dangers of unknown waters. Long before England became a really maritime nation the Spaniards had crossed and re-crossed the Atlantic, had sailed their stately ships over the waters of the Pacific, and had explored the Indies; thus gathering confidence in their own prowess, and perhaps a spice of contempt for more stay-at-home people.

These two causes—religion and trade—widened the breach more and more between England and Spain. Elizabeth, fully realising the vast extent of Philip's power, laboured hard, earnestly, and for a long time successfully, to avert open war between the two countries. She could not, however—or at least she did not—prevent the bolder of her subjects from despoiling the Spaniards whenever they found opportunity.

When the people of the Netherlands rose, under William of Orange, against the tyranny of Alva, Philip's general in the Low Countries, numbers of young Englishmen, many belonging to rich and noble families, risked their lives in order to assist the Netherland Protestants. In the terrible and unequal fight waged by the stubborn Dutchmen, these reckless adventurers took a full share, gaining a splendid reputation as brave and heroic soldiers, equally ready to undergo the most arduous toils, and to face the enemy on the most deadly battlefields.

At sea, too, they displayed similar qualities, and learned to pit themselves with no small degree of success against the haughty Dons who had hitherto brooked no masters.

Among the crowd of able and gallant men who leaped to the front during the reign of Elizabeth, none made a more enduring name than Francis Drake. The date of this skilful adventurer's birth is somewhat uncertain, though it is probable that he was born either in 1539 or in 1541.

According to the usual narrative, his father was a Devonshire man, who, on account of religious persecution, left his native county and fled to Kent, where, it is said, he read prayers to the naval seamen and was afterwards ordained Deacon. Be this as it may, young Drake was apprenticed to the master of a barque, in which he made coasting voyages, and even ventured to Zealand and France.

It will thus be seen that Drake began at the very lowest step of the ladder up which he was to climb so high, and it is pleasing to learn that from the first he displayed some of those admirable traits for which he was afterwards so famous. He laboured hard and faithfully in his master's service, proving both honest and diligent; so much so, that, when the owner of the barque died, he left his ship to the youthful sailor.

At that time, one of the foremost seamen in England was Captain John Hawkins, whom we remember chiefly as a trafficker in negro slaves; though, as Paymaster of the Navy, he had much to do with organising the fleet that baffled the Spanish Armada.

In 1567, Hawkins was preparing for a further voyage to the West Indies, and, acting on his advice, Drake sold his barque and bought a small ship—the *Judith*—to join in the adventure. Though still a young man, he had gained great experience of the sea, and had caught the adventurous spirit of the period. The New World with its storehouse of treasures was a powerful magnet, and the chance of a brush with the Spaniards only added to the attraction which the voyage had for youthful minds.

In October 1567, the expedition started. Present-day sailors would stand aghast at the idea of ploughing the troubled waters of the Atlantic in such flimsy craft, but these rough old rovers were as ready to brave the storms of the ocean as the cannon-balls of the Spaniards.

Elizabeth had lent Hawkins the *Jesus of Lubeck*, a royal vessel of 700 tons, and this was the leviathan of the squadron. The other vessels, besides two very small craft, the *Angel* and the *Swallow*, were the *Minion*, the *William and John*, and the *Judith*. The voyage began disastrously, a storm off Cape Finisterre destroying all the boats and nearly disabling the ships.

However, the adventurers reached Cape Verde, where, after much hard fighting, they succeeded in capturing one hundred and fifty negroes, and, proceeding along the coast of Guinea, they procured two hundred and fifty more, though not without the loss of several of their own men. The subject is an unpleasant one; but it is only fair to state that, in those days, very few people saw any evil in the slave-trade, and Hawkins and Drake were neither better nor worse than their neighbours.

With their cargoes of human beings the ships sailed for the Spanish West Indies, touching at one place and another, and disposing of the slaves as best they could. Terrible storms, however, one of which nearly wrecked the *Jesus,* drove them from their course, and they were compelled to run for safety into the port of San Juan d'Ulloa, in the Bay of Mexico.

Having escaped from the perils of the sea, the squadron was soon in danger from the Spaniards. The port was guarded by a battery on a small island, and twelve large ships lay at anchor in the haven; while the next morning a Spanish fleet of thirteen warships appeared in the offing. Hawkins was in a desperate position, but he faced it with a boldness which shows clearly what manner of men these sturdy forefathers of ours were.

Sending a message to the Spanish admiral, he coolly informed him that on certain conditions he would permit him to bring his vessels into port. These conditions were that the English should have liberty to trade and to buy provisions, and to keep possession, during their stay, of the island with its battery. The treaty was signed, the hostile fleet entered the harbour, and the Spaniards, as Hawkins had half expected, immediately began to plan how best to overwhelm their audacious foe.

Numbers of soldiers were secretly put on board the Spanish ships: others were so placed that they could capture the island by a swift attack, and a huge hulk filled with hidden men was moored alongside the *Minion.* Some English sailors who had gone ashore were treacherously seized; and suddenly, at the sound of a trumpet, three hundred fighting-men poured from the hulk on to the *Minion's* deck.

But the Spaniards, with all their advantages, discovered they had undertaken no easy task. The crew of the *Minion* stuck to their posts; Hawkins, with his brave fellows, rushed to aid them; a desperate conflict ensued, and the assailants were flung overboard, until not one, except the dead and wounded, remained on the stout little English craft.

Meanwhile the battle raged furiously in every direction. The guns from the island sent their shot crashing into the English ships; the Spanish galleons cannonaded them; fire-ships enveloped in flames were sent drifting towards them; but not a man flinched from the unequal encounter. Again and again, the enemy were beaten off. Two of their vessels were sunk, and one was burned; but the island guns continued to work havoc on the English squadron, nor was there any means of silencing them.

At last, the *Jesus of Lubeck* was so crippled as to be rendered utterly unfit for sailing. Her mainmast was tottering to a fall; her foremast was snapped asunder by a chain-shot; her hull was riddled like a sieve—and she was, indeed, reduced to a hopeless wreck. Then, and then only, did Hawkins and his crew abandon her and row in their pinnaces to the *Minion,* when a favourable breeze enabled that battered ship to creep out of the harbour.

The condition of the survivors on the *Minion* was still far from enviable. The ship was sadly damaged, and the provisions were so scarce that the miserable sailors were glad to eat dogs, cats, rats, monkeys, parrots, and even hides. Some began to murmur, until their leader permitted all those who wished it to go ashore farther down the coast, to shift for themselves.

Then the prow of the *Minion* was turned homeward. But misfortune followed misfortune : furious storms threatened to dash the crazy craft to the bottom ; the crew, worn out by hard toil and privation, and weakened by scanty provisions, sickened and died, till there were barely enough left to navigate the vessel to Mount's Bay, where, in January 1568, she dropped anchor.

The *Judith,* having weathered a stormy and perilous voyage, had arrived some time previously, never having been in company of the *Minion* after the close of the fight. Just what part the youthful Drake played in the memorable contest is difficult to say, though we cannot doubt that he acted as became a brave and gallant Englishman. Hawkins does not mention his name, but Job Hartop, one of the unfortunate sailors captured by the Spaniards, says : " Our general willed Mr. Francis Drake to come in with the *Judith* and lay the *Minion* aboard, to take in men and other things needful, and then to go out, and so he did."

Of one thing we are sure : Drake never forgave the Spaniards for their treacherous attack at San Juan d' Ulloa. From that time onward until the day of his death he remained their most resolute and determined enemy, holding stoutly to the opinion that he was justified in recouping himself, with interest, for the loss they had inflicted upon him.

CHAPTER II.

A Daring Enterprise.

WE have said in the preceding chapter that Queen Elizabeth, although unwilling to break openly with Philip of Spain, was always ready, when it could be done without endangering the peace of the country, to encourage her adventurous subjects in their efforts to obtain a portion of the Spanish trade.

And this, even without the goodwill of their sovereign, hundreds of Englishmen cheerfully attempted—nor could the chance of imprisonment, loss of property, or even loss of life hold them in check. The evils they encountered only made them the more eager to proceed, and this was well shown in the career of Francis Drake. Ruined at San Juan d' Ulloa, and only narrowly escaping death, he nevertheless set about the preparations for another venture.

It seems, indeed, as if, after his disastrous voyage with Hawkins, he resolved to devote his life and what wealth he possessed to harassing the Spaniards; and we find that he went about his purpose in a very cool and business-like manner. With two small ships, the *Dragon* and the *Swanne,* he sailed to the West Indies in 1570, and the following year made another voyage in the *Swanne* with the express object of obtaining information which would stand him in good service for his next venture.

This, which is generally (though wrongly) called his third voyage, began in May 1572, and the description of the squadron which he considered sufficient to undertake so mighty an enterprise fills us with wonder. His own ship, the *Pacha of Plymouth,* was only of 70 tons burden, while the *Swanne,* commanded by his brother John, was of 25 tons. The crews numbered 73; but there was a goodly store of weapons, while the vessels carried three pinnaces constructed in such a manner that they could be put together or taken asunder just as was needed.

The main object of the voyage was to attack and plunder the city of Nombre de Dios, the storehouse of the West, where the gold obtained by the Spaniards from Mexico and Peru was kept until it could be despatched to Europe.

At a place named by Drake on one of his former voyages, Port Pheasant, the sailors encountered a friendly warning. On a plate of lead which had been attached to a high tree another adventurer had engraved these words :—

"CAPTAIN DRAKE,—If you fortune to come into this port, make haste away; for the Spaniards which you had with you here last year have betrayed this place, and taken away all that you left here. I departed hence this present July 7, 1572.—Your very loving friend,   JOHN GARRET."

Drake, however, had come too far to be

frightened by a shadow; so he dropped anchor, and, selecting a suitable piece of ground, proceeded to erect a kind of stockade. The next day, while fitting up his pinnaces, he was surprised by the arrival of an English ship commanded by Captain James Rause, and the two adventurers agreed to make common cause.

Leaving Rause to guard the ships, Drake departed with four pinnaces, and, after a visit to the Isle of Pinos, appeared before Nombre de Dios. It was about three o'clock in the morning when the daring band leaped on shore and gained possession of the battery guarding the bay. Very soon, however, the sleeping town sprang to life: the church-bell rolled out its clangorous alarm; the war-drums were beaten; muskets were discharged at random; and the soldiers added to the babel of sounds by hoarse shouts that the enemy were upon them.

But, although taken partly by surprise, the garrison presented a bold front and assembled in the market-place. Leaving twelve men to guard the boats, the impetuous Drake pushed ahead, but, unfortunately, received a dangerous wound in the leg. This for a while he concealed from his followers, and gallantly led them to the governor's house, where they discovered a huge heap of silver. Thence they made their way to the king's treasure-house, Drake heartening the rovers by saying he had now brought them to the mouth of the treasury of the world; which, if they did not gain, none but themselves could be blamed.

S.D.   B

Leaving his brother and John Oxenham (so well known to the countless readers of "Westward Ho!") to break open the treasure-house, Drake advanced to the market-place with a portion of his company, to hold the Spaniards in check. But, intrepid as was his spirit, it could not prevail longer against the loss of blood : his head became dizzy ; his sight failed ; he stumbled forward painfully, and it became evident to his men that he had barely sufficient strength to stand. They begged him to return to the pinnace ; but, unwilling to acknowledge himself beaten, he refused, whereupon they carried him aboard.

The disaster to Drake brought about the failure of the attack, though several of the sailors succeeded in securing a fair amount of booty, while a Spanish ship in the harbour was captured and her cargo of wine transferred to the boats. Then, sailing to an island, the rovers remained there to afford the injured a chance of recovering from their troublesome wounds.

On their return to the Isle of Pinos, Captain Rause decided that, now their presence was known, it was too risky to remain on the coast, so he sailed away; but Drake resolved to hazard an attempt on Cartagena, hoping to recoup himself for the loss already sustained. It would never do, he argued, to return to England without having first spoiled the enemy.

Making prizes as he voyaged, he sailed with his two ships toward the town, and there, manning his pinnaces, led them into the harbour. His only booty, however, was a large vessel from Seville ;

for the garrison, fore-warned of his coming, had
made every preparation to give him a warm
reception. Companies, both of cavalry and of
infantry, were drawn up along the shore, while
thirty large cannon were loaded and trained on
the landing-place.

Perceiving that a surprise was out of the
question, Drake returned to his ships, to consider
his plans anew. He had no intention of abandoning the object of his voyage, and yet he found
himself in a difficult position. After setting aside
a sufficient guard for his vessels, he had not
enough sailors to man the pinnaces. In this
dilemma, he resolved upon a startling stroke—no
less a plan than scuttling the *Swanne*.

Sending for the carpenter of that ship, he
ordered him to go down secretly in the middle
of the night into the well of the vessel, and to
bore three holes as near to the keel as possible.
At first the carpenter refused, declaring that if he
were found out his shipmates would most certainly
kill him; but, on being told his leader's reasons,
he consented.

The next day the *Swanne* was discovered to
be full of water. The sailors, who loved their
ship, began to work with a will—some toiling
at the pumps, others endeavouring to find the
leak, and all thoroughly astonished at the
unexpected accident. But the carpenter had performed his task well, and, in spite of every effort,
the water rose so rapidly that it was impossible
to save the vessel. Then, by Drake's advice,
the crew removed their goods to the *Pacha,* and

burned the leaky ship to prevent her from falling into the hands of the Spaniards. By this strange method, Drake was enabled to obtain sufficient men to sail his pinnaces.

In order to throw the Spaniards off the scent, he now sailed to the Sound of Darien, anchored his vessel in a retired spot, where she would not easily be observed, and, with the assistance of the natives, cleared a piece of ground on which several houses were built for the accommodation of the sailors. After a stay of fifteen days, Drake once more made an expedition with his three pinnaces; but, although he captured several ships, nothing could be done at Cartagena, where the Spaniards were found well prepared.

The hardships and privations endured in the boats now brought on a dangerous sickness, of which one man died; while others were so enfeebled that it became necessary to return to the *Pacha,* where Drake was met by the sad tidings that his brother John had been killed while attempting to board a Spanish frigate.

This heavy blow was quickly followed by another: sickness again broke out; six of the sailors died within two or three days, and among them was Joseph Drake, who died in his brother's arms. But Drake possessed an iron will, and even this sad calamity could not turn him from his purpose.

He now resolved to travel overland to Panama, and, with eighteen of his own men and thirty natives, he began his march, hoping to surprise one of the numerous companies which travelled

"Drake gazed with awe at the waters."

with the King of Spain's treasures to the ports.
But misfortune had not yet finished with him,
and, owing to the folly of a drunken sailor, he
missed his prize.

The overland expedition, however, had one
great and notable result. On the summit of a
high hill stood a large tree, from which it was
possible to obtain a view of the Pacific Ocean.
Climbing the tree, Drake gazed with awe and
wonder at the famous waters, of which he had
frequently heard; and, in the words of an old
writer, he besought God "to give him life and
leave, once to sail an English ship in those seas."
Thenceforth Captain Drake was never to rest
content until he had steered a vessel across the
broad waters of the mighty Pacific. It was a
memorable day, not only in the life of Drake,
but also in the history of England.

On their journey back to the coast the sailors
fell in with a treasure party, and helped themselves
to all the bars of gold and silver they could carry.
This slice of good fortune seemed likely to be
followed by a disaster; for, on approaching the
coast, they saw not their own boats, but several
Spanish pinnaces. Their situation was now
critical, but Drake extricated them from it by a
daring venture.

Causing a raft to be made with fallen trees,
he chose three picked men to accompany him,
and boldly started to search for his pinnaces.
For six hours these hardy fellows sailed about
on their crazy craft, sitting up to their waists in
water, and in danger every moment of being

washed off. But the men who voyaged with Drake had need to be fearless, and to be capable of facing danger of every possible kind. Fortunately, this novel trip ended in complete success; the pinnaces were discovered, and the remainder of the company, with the treasure, having been brought off, the whole party returned in safety to their frigate.

Drake now acknowledged that it was useless to remain longer in the neighbourhood. Many of his men had died of disease, or had been slain in skirmishes with the enemy, and there was no likelihood of the Spaniards being taken by surprise. Accordingly, he resolved to return home, and, having rewarded the natives who had served him so faithfully, he weighed anchor and started on the voyage to England.

The expedition does not appear to have resulted in a great success, except that the adventurers acquired a fair amount of booty; but when we consider the magnitude of the task, we are lost in wonder at the audacity of the man who, with such scanty means, boldly undertook so hazardous an enterprise.

The homeward voyage passed without adventure, and, on August 9, 1573, Drake once more dropped anchor in Plymouth Sound. It was Sunday, and the worthy citizens were assembled in church; but, at the cry that the famous rover had arrived, nearly every one trooped down to the quay to welcome the captain and his crew, who had survived so many dangers.

It was a triumphant home-coming for Drake;

but his joy must have been tempered by regret that some who had started out with him so full of confidence had fallen by the way, and were sleeping their last long sleep in a hostile and far-off land.

CHAPTER III.

In the Wake of Magellan.

THE most marvellous of all Drake's voyages did not begin until five years after his return from Panama ; but during that time he had by no means been idle. Ireland was aflame with strife and rebellion, and the young and brilliant Earl of Essex was appointed Governor of Ulster, with the object of crushing the rebels. This he expected to accomplish by means of volunteers, who were to be rewarded for their services by grants of land in the province.

Essex had already befriended Drake, who now hastened to the assistance of his patron with three small vessels which he had manned and fitted out at his own expense. The records of this portion of his career are rather meagre, but we learn that he did excellent service and took a prominent share in the capture of several strong forts. Essex, however, did not succeed in sub-duing Ulster, being hampered by his powerful enemy, the Earl of Leicester, and, in despair at his failure, he resigned his command.

Drake's proved ability in the Irish war, how-ever, led to an introduction to the Queen, and we are told that the haughty sovereign treated the gallant rover with marked favour. This is probably true, as he was exactly the kind of man she delighted to encourage. He was brave, daring, resolute, and absolutely without fear; he hated the Spaniards, and was ever ready to strike a blow against them; he was willing to risk his life cheerfully in her service, and, while he harassed her enemies, she felt assured that he was able to make his hand guard his head.

For it must be understood that men like Drake did not sail the seas with the might of England at their back. They were simply private adventurers, and, when Philip of Spain caught them, he had a perfect right to hang them up by the heels. Elizabeth dared not admit they acted under her orders, for that would have provoked a war which England was not powerful enough to wage. But the Queen was a far-seeing woman, who recognised that every successful venture to the Spanish Main increased the strength of England while it weakened that of Spain. So she flattered these rough old Sea-Dogs with a gracious smile, and a courtly phrase which had little meaning, and in return they gladly imperilled both liberty and life.

During this interval, Drake had been secretly laying his plans for one of the most memorable voyages in the world's history. The vow he had made on the occasion of his first glimpse of the Pacific had not been forgotten; and the time was now fast approaching for its fulfilment.

In November 1577, his squadron was ready. The largest vessel was the *Pelican,* in which the leader himself sailed, and this was only of 100 tons burden : the crews of the entire squadron numbered one hundred and sixty-three seamen.

The dangers of the ocean in themselves rendered the voyage a bold and hazardous undertaking, but there were other perils also to be faced. This handful of men was about to venture into a region claimed by the Spaniards as their sole property, and the subjects of King Philip were not over-scrupulous in their methods of upholding their claim. Truly, when the few Englishmen unmoored their craft in Plymouth harbour on that dark November morning, they took their lives in their hands.

The start was not of such a nature as to raise their spirits. A fierce storm damaged their vessels and drove them back to Plymouth to refit. But the crews were picked men, and the disaster did not daunt them. On December 13th they made another start, and, destroying several Spanish vessels on their route, arrived in safety at Porto Praya, where they seized a Portuguese ship with a valuable cargo.

Now among the volunteers who accompanied the expedition was a certain Thomas Doughty. We know little about him except that he was a friend of Drake, who put him in charge of the prize. We cannot be sure how this unfortunate man incurred the displeasure of his shipmates, but in a short time they accused him of secreting some of the captured valuables for his own use ;

so he was deposed from his command, and Thomas Drake appointed in his stead.

Probably the incident was a trifling one, as Drake, who wished to remain in the prize, sent Doughty to take charge of the *Pelican*. Here again he fell into disfavour, by—according to Mr. Fletcher, the clergyman on board—"taking upon him too great a command." On this occasion Drake transferred him, as a prisoner in disgrace, to the flyboat.

Near the equator the ships were becalmed for nearly three weeks; but finally, after a slow and tedious voyage, they reached Brazil, and, having procured a supply of water and provisions, stood to the southward. Everything was new and strange to the hardy mariners, who gazed with astonishment at the novel sights, and the natives whom they met.

In June 1578, they anchored in Port St. Julian, where the famous Portuguese explorer had landed seventy years before and had left a gibbet on which some of his men had been hanged for mutiny. Strangely enough, it was fated that, at this very place, a member of Drake's expedition should lose his life. The story has been told many times, but it is scarcely likely that the whole truth will ever be known.

Camden, the historian, writes: "John Doughty, an industrious and stout man, and the next unto Drake, was called to his trial for raising a mutiny in the fleet, found guilty by twelve men after the English manner, and condemned to death, which he suffered undauntedly, being beheaded, having first received the Holy Communion with Drake. And, indeed, the most impartial persons in the fleet were of opinion that he had acted seditiously. Yet wanted there not some, who, pretending to understand things better than others, gave out that Drake had it in charge from Leicester to take off Doughty, upon any pretence whatsoever, because he had reported abroad that the Earl of Essex was made away by the cunning practices of Leicester."

Other writers declare that Doughty confessed his guilt; but Mr. Fletcher, who states that he was accused by his enemies "for words spoken by him to them, being in England, in the Governor's garden at Plymouth, long before our departure thence," continues : "How true it was wherewith they charged him upon their oath, I know not; but he utterly denied it, upon his salvation, at the hour of communicating the Sacrament of the body and blood of Christ, at the hour and moment of his death, affirming that he was innocent of such things whereof he was accused, judged, and suffered death for."

How a single man, without friends, could have expected to raise a successful mutiny against a leader, beloved by almost every one in the fleet, is difficult to imagine ; yet we cannot believe that Drake would have sacrificed his comrade without just cause.

The writer of the "World Encompassed," who is generally supposed to have been Thomas Drake, pens a graphic account of the closing scenes in this grim tragedy.

"The General himself communicated in this sacred ordinance (the Sacrament) with this condemned, penitent gentleman, who showed great tokens of a contrite and repentant heart. After this holy repast they dined also at the same table together, as cheerfully in sobriety, as ever in their lives they had done aforetime, each cheering up the other, as if some journey only had been in hand."

It is, indeed, a most strange and startling picture, this of the two men—one the judge, the other a condemned prisoner—quietly dining together and pledging each other in wine, while preparations were being made outside for the swift and sudden execution of one of those who thus sat at meat. And further, we are informed in the narrative that, the repast being ended, "Mr. Doughty came forth and kneeled down, preparing at once his neck for the axe, and his spirit for heaven, which having done, without long ceremony, as one who had before digested this whole tragedy, he desired all the rest to pray for him, and willed the executioner to do his office, not to fear nor spare."

And thus, whatever his crimes or his follies may have been, Thomas Doughty went to his death calmly and peacefully, as a gallant English gentleman should, showing no fear, and was buried in that lonely, far-off land, away from kith and kin and from the land of his birth, with only a common stone to mark the place of his burial. It is altogether a sad and mournful story, and, somehow, one cannot help feeling that, without casting any reflection on Drake, it throws a dark and deep shadow across the glory of this famous expedition.

The long delay at Port St. Julian began seriously to reduce the stock of provisions; the sailors had but scanty rations, and were often sore put to it to procure a satisfying meal. Small mussels were anxiously searched for and eagerly gathered, while certain seaweeds, when cooked in primitive fashion, were regarded by the crew as an exquisite delicacy.

At last, Drake decided to resume the voyage, and, having broken up one of his ships which had sprung a leak, he led the remaining three— the *Pelican,* the *Elizabeth,* and the *Marigold*—still farther southward, reaching the Strait of Magellan on August 20th.

In 1520, Ferdinand Magellan, a Portuguese navigator in the service of Spain, had, first of all European explorers, discovered this passage leading from the Atlantic to the Pacific. His voyage had been full of perils: some of his officers had mutinied; his vessels had been shattered by tempestuous storms—one had been dashed to pieces against the iron-bound coast. In spite of these disasters, Magellan, resolute and undismayed, had pushed on, determined to navigate this mysterious waterway.

The grim and barren rocks on each side of him threatened destruction to his frail vessels; the mighty seas appeared ready to engulf them; but Magellan, with splendid intrepidity, sailed onward, and, after encountering many terrific perils, safely reached the broad ocean to which he gave the name of Pacific.

And now an Englishman had come, with a still smaller squadron, to repeat the daring feat. Always mindful of the glory of his sovereign, he ordered his men to strike their topsails in her honour; and then, willing to show respect to his own patron, he changed the name of his ship to the *Golden Hind,* that being Sir Christopher Hatton's badge. Nor did he forget to hold a solemn service of thanksgiving for all the mercies which had been vouchsafed to him during the first part of his long and hazardous voyage. Then with a stout heart he began to explore the difficult passage which lay between him and his coveted goal.

It was a risky undertaking, and the sailors might well have been excused had their courage failed as they viewed the rocky cliffs which seemed to encompass them. Other dangers, too, abounded. The channel was narrow and studded with rocks; there was no chart, and the officers had, as it were, to grope their way slowly and painfully along. All around the scene was wild and weird, and calculated to strike terror into the hearts of the beholders. On each side mighty peaks towered to the skies, their tops surmounted by snow, while on the left lay the desolate island of Fuego.

In spite of every danger, however, the squadron passed through the Strait in sixteen days, when a wild storm drove them southward, and the *Marigold,* parting company with her consorts, disappeared, never to be seen again. The *Pelican* and the *Elizabeth* managed to find shelter in a bay; but, soon after dropping their anchors, the storm burst upon them with redoubled fury— the *Pelican's* cable parted, and Drake was driven out to sea.

Captain Winter, left to himself, appears to have had no stomach for further adventures, and, sorely against the wishes of his crew, he sailed back through the Strait and home to England, where, upon his arrival, Drake and his companions were given up for lost.

CHAPTER IV.

A Marvellous Voyage.

IT must be remembered that Drake was not yet aware either of the *Marigold's* loss or of Captain Winter's desertion. Like a prudent leader, he had arranged, in case the vessels were separated, the latitude and longitude in which they should meet, and he cheered his men's spirits by predicting that at the proper time they would be rejoined by their comrades.

Meanwhile, his calamities were not at an end. His pinnace, manned by eight sailors, was blown during a hurricane out of sight of the ship. The poor fellows had only one day's provisions, but, by a lucky accident, they reached the Straits. Their sufferings were intense; they had no food beyond penguin meat, but, incredible as it may appear, they succeeded in reaching the Rio de la Plata. Here six ventured into the woods for the purpose of procuring provisions, and were attacked by the Indians, who wounded them all with poisoned arrows and captured four. The others rejoined their comrades in the boat, but soon died, while the pinnace was dashed to pieces against the rocks of an island.

Of the eight men, two only now remained alive, and so intense was their misery for want of food and water, that, braving the dangers of the ocean, they paddled back to the mainland on a plank. Half crazy with thirst they hurried to a stream, where one, over-drinking himself, died, and was buried by his distracted comrade. It is pleasant to recall that the solitary survivor lived to reach his native country.

But now we must return to the intrepid captain of the *Golden Hind,* alone on the broad bosom of an unknown sea, with his consorts missing and with his own crew sadly reduced in numbers. The situation was enough to appal the stoutest heart; but Drake, though fully aware of the perils surrounding him, refused to be cast down. The tempest drove him far to the southward; his ship was beset by dangerous rocks; he had no chart and no knowledge of his position; he could not find a place in which to anchor, and the leaping seas tossed his half-manned vessel about as if she had been a cockle-shell.

But the steadfast sailor battled with the storm-tossed ocean as he had striven with his human foes. Beaten back time after time, he clung to his

" Drake himself narrowly escaped death."

resolution, and at length Fortune, as if wearied
by his obstinacy, relented, and with a favourable
breeze he sailed to the latitude where he expected
to find the remaining vessels of his squadron. In
this, of course, he was unsuccessful, as one lay at
the bottom of the sea, and the other was fast
speeding to England.

Even this disappointment could not crush Drake's
spirit, and death alone had the power to break his
iron resolution. The perils of the ocean were
now replaced by the hostility of the natives. At
the island of Macho he found some Indians, to
whom he gave several small presents, and they
in return showed him where to obtain a much-
needed supply of water. But their friendly feelings
suddenly vanished.

On the landing party going ashore with their
casks, they were attacked by some five hundred
natives with a stinging volley of arrows which
slew the two foremost sailors outright and wounded
all the others. Drake himself narrowly escaped
death, being wounded by two arrows, one of
which pierced his face just under the right eye.
It is very probable that the Indians, hearing one
of the sailors pronounce the word *Aqua* for water,
concluded that the whole party were Spaniards,
and seized this opportunity to take a slight
vengeance for the cruelties that had been committed upon themselves.

At a place on the mainland, where the wanderers
afterwards landed, they were discovered by the
Spaniards, and one man, who either could not or
would not retreat to the boat in time, was shot.

Drake, who had not yet abandoned all hope of meeting with his missing consorts, now cast anchor in a quiet harbour, and fitted up a pinnace with the object of searching the creeks on the coast, thinking that in this way he might obtain some information. And now, at various places, the startled Spaniards saw with amazement, this little band of hardy adventurers coolly taking possession of the bars of silver, which had been collected for export to Spain.

Perhaps the most remarkable of these bold enterprises was their unopposed entrance into Callao, the port of Lima. The harbour was crowded with shipping, no fewer than seventeen vessels being laden with valuable cargoes. Drake's appearance was something of a miracle to the Spaniards, who never dreamed that an English ship was sailing in these forbidden seas.

But, even when we make allowance for this surprise, it is hard to believe that they never struck a blow in defence of their treasure, but allowed the detested Englishmen to collect fifteen hundred bars of silver, a large chest filled with money, and other valuables. This, however, they did, watching from the shore in hopeless impotency the audacious sea-rovers calmly transferring their plunder to the *Golden Hind*.

Fortune, hitherto so chary of her favours, now smiled on the English leader, who learned that the *Cacafuego,* a stately galleon, laden with gold and silver, had recently sailed from the harbour on a voyage to Panama. This was fine news for Drake, who started off at full speed in the direction of Panama, leaving the half-dazed Spaniards to deplore their losses.

With every stitch of canvas spread, the *Golden Hind* bounded on her northern course, while the adventurers, forgetful of previous hardships and miseries, rejoiced over the plunder they had secured, and looked forward with light hearts to largely increasing their booty. In this expectation they were not disappointed. An unfortunate brigantine, with eighty pounds of gold and a number of emeralds forming part of her cargo, came across their path and was promptly rifled, while a few days afterwards the stately *Cacafuego* herself was sighted.

And here again we find another marvel in this marvellous voyage. The *Golden Hind* was a small vessel of 100 tons, and battered by a succession of tempests ; her sailors were few in number, and worn-out by toil and disease. The *Cacafuego*, on the other hand, was a massive galleon, well armed and manned by a full crew. An ordinary man might be excused for thinking that Drake was about to catch a Tartar ; but the commander of the *Golden Hind* was very far from being an ordinary person.

With all the assurance in the world, he ran up alongside his gigantic opponent, opened fire with his guns, knocked away one of the galleon's masts, called to his boarders to follow, leaped on to the enemy's deck, drove the astonished sailors before him, and compelled them to strike their flag. With ludicrous ease he had made himself master of the galleon, which the Spaniards called "the great glory of the South Sea." Pearls and precious stones, gold and silver bars, and chests of money were speedily transferred to the *Golden Hind,* the value of the treasure being reckoned at £90,000.

Steering clear of Panama, Drake continued his voyage northward, and, having plundered another vessel on the way, arrived at Aguapilca, where he obtained more booty in the shape of gold and jewels, as well as a stock of provisions. Here, too, discovering a vessel going south, he entrusted the master with a letter to Captain Winter, who, he supposed, was still beating about somewhere in the Pacific Ocean.

The daring sailor now began to think of a return home, and the more so, perhaps, as his sailors showed a considerable anxiety as to the future. But his very success had placed him in a difficult position. The only route known to him was by way of Magellan's Strait, and he argued that the Spaniards would not allow him to pass through that channel unopposed. He had plundered their galleons and sacked their towns. His ship was laden with stolen treasure; her very presence was a deadly insult to those who called themselves masters of the Pacific: it was hardly likely that they would permit him to depart quietly with his booty.

But might it not be possible to return by way of the north-east? In his condition, with a single ship, a handful of men, and these enfeebled by toil and privation, it would certainly be a most dangerous undertaking; but Drake determined to try. Contrary winds, however, drove him southward, and, his vessel having sprung a leak, he put into a harbour, which is supposed to have been what is now known as the port of San Francisco. Some of the stores were disembarked, and tents set up on shore for the crew.

Here Drake remained for five weeks, being treated with the greatest kindness and respect by the natives, who, according to the old accounts, regarded him as a god. It is reported they made him their king; but however that may be, he took possession of the country in the name of Queen Elizabeth, and gave it the name of New Albion.

Drake now abandoned his intention of trying to discover a north-east passage, and, having obtained a chart of the Pacific from a Spanish sailor, he decided on sailing to the Philippines, and set out towards the end of July. For sixty-eight days the little vessel pursued her lonely way, and then, to the huge delight of all on board, she came in sight of islands, supposed by later writers to be the Pellew Islands.

Thence after an encounter with the natives, Drake steered for the Philippines and dropped anchor at Ternate, the capital of the Moluccas. Here his men were received with kindness, and the natives were very favourably impressed by Drake's fair and even generous dealing. The next stopping-place was a small island off Celebes, where the sailors landed, and, erecting tents, made a stay of several weeks.

Thus far, all had gone well with the daring

explorers; but on the night of January 9, 1580, the *Golden Hind* struck a rock, where she remained firmly set. At the first streak of dawn the anxious mariners endeavoured to get the vessel off; but all their efforts were futile, and it appeared almost certain that the *Golden Hind,* filled with the Spanish treasure, would become a total wreck, and that the toil-worn adventurers would find a watery grave. A solemn prayer for safety was offered up by the distressed sailors, who fully expected that every minute would be their last.

The *Golden Hind,* however, remained firmly wedged, and, as a last resort, Drake issued orders for the vessel to be lightened. Three tons of cloves, taken aboard at Ternate, were thrown into the sea; and then, with extreme reluctance, the crew sacrificed eight of their guns, and a quantity of meal and beans. Still the *Golden Hind* did not move, but when the tide turned she slipped off most unexpectedly into deep water.

With joyful hearts the men resumed their voyage, and at Java they were supplied most liberally with provisions by the natives, who, for the space of a fortnight, helped their strange guests to pass the time in feasting and merriment. But now the wanderers began to tire of the tedious journey; they longed to see the white cliffs of the old home from which they had been so long absent, and, setting sail once more, they rounded the Cape of Good Hope, running straight on to Sierra Leone, where they landed to obtain water and to secure a supply of fruit.

On September 26, 1580, nearly three years after her first setting forth, the *Golden Hind*, bruised and battered by storm and tempest, sailed proudly into Plymouth Sound with her gallant crew and intrepid captain, who had fearlessly braved so many perils by sea and land, and who, by their daring and successful voyage, had brought no small honour to their native country.

CHAPTER V.

The Luck Turns:

THE arrival of the *Golden Hind* at Plymouth was welcomed with every expression of pleasure and delight. The joy of the inhabitants was unbounded, as, after the return of Captain Winter, they had abandoned all expectation of ever greeting Drake and his comrades again. The mayor and the principal citizens hurried to the quay to meet the weary explorers; joy-bells pealed, and dense crowds cheered lustily as their favourite hero appeared in sight. Feasting and merriment was the order of the day, and men told each other proudly of the brave deeds performed by these west-country heroes.

From Plymouth, Drake sailed to London, where his fame had already preceded him. First of all Englishmen, he had voyaged round the world, and had returned safely with fabulous wealth, taken from the national enemy. The people, blunt and outspoken, vigorously applauded his exploits, but those in higher stations were slow and cautious in expressing approval.

Some even spoke harsh and bitter words, styling him the "master-thief of the unknown world," and declaring that he had not come by his treasure honestly. The Queen herself, who had sanctioned his enterprise and had sent him forth with gracious words, remained silent, and it seemed not unlikely that the daring navigator would see the inside of an English prison.

The truth is that the Queen's advisers were frightened by his success. As the wonderful incidents of the voyage became known, their alarm increased, and they feared lest the King of Spain should plunge the country into war. And truly, Philip might have pleaded ample cause for stern measures. His towns had been sacked, his soldiers slain, and his galleons plundered of their costly treasures on the high seas. And all this had been done by a hated Englishman, who could show no more authority for his deeds than could an ordinary pirate.

The cautious statesmen who held power under Elizabeth pointed out these matters forcibly to their royal mistress, saying that, if she showed favour to Drake, the King of Spain would be right in considering that the expedition had been undertaken with the royal sanction.

Elizabeth hesitated, and we can well believe that she turned the subject over in her mind many times before deciding what to do. She feared Spain, and had no desire for war; she did not wish to lose the results of Drake's

"She bestowed on him the honour of knighthood."

enterprise. He had struck a stout blow at the Spaniards, and his ship was filled with priceless treasures. The wealth he had acquired proved too strong a temptation. Elizabeth could not find it in her heart to return this store of gold and silver and precious stones to the lawful owners ; so Drake, after waiting five months in doubt, received the information that her Majesty intended to do him honour.

Accordingly, on April 4, 1581, Elizabeth, having dined at Deptford, proceeded in royal state to the weather-beaten barque which had passed successfully through so many adventures, and there, in the midst of a brilliant company, she bestowed on the fearless sailor the honour of knighthood, making him Sir Francis Drake. She also commanded that the *Golden Hind* should be preserved as a memorial of his striking achievement ; and for many years it lay in Deptford Dock, where it was visited by thousands of admiring people. At length, when the old ship could no longer be repaired, the best of the wood was fashioned into a chair and presented to the University of Oxford.

After Elizabeth's visit to the *Golden Hind* there were few men who dared to call Drake's doings into question. He became the popular idol, and his name spread throughout the kingdom as that of the most fearless and the most skilful mariner in the world.

But, as had been expected, Philip of Spain was not in the humour to overlook the injury done to his subjects, and Mendoza, the Spanish ambassador in London, received orders to demand the booty, and to insist on the punishment of the bold rover. Now Elizabeth, as we have shown, was a cautious and wary ruler, who, for numerous reasons, was unwilling to offend her powerful rival; but she quickly recognised when it was necessary to stand firm even against Philip himself.

The reply which she returned was worthy of both herself and the English people. " The Spaniards," she wrote, "by the ill-treatment of her subjects, to whom they had prohibited commerce contrary to the law of nations, had drawn these mischiefs upon themselves. Drake should be forthcoming to answer according to law, if he were convicted by good evidence and testimony to have committed anything against law and right. The goods in question were purposely laid by, that satisfaction might be made to the Spaniards, though the Queen had spent a greater sum of money than Drake had brought in, against those rebels whom the Spaniards had raised against her. Moreover, she understood not why her or any other prince's subjects should be debarred from the Indies, which she could not persuade herself the Spaniards had any just title to. Neither," she continued, "can a title to the ocean belong to any people, or private persons; forasmuch as neither nature nor public use and custom permitted any possession thereof."

Drake was ordered to restore a certain sum belonging to private persons; but Elizabeth kept tight hold of the bulk of the treasure, the major portion of which was afterwards divided among the adventurers and those who had borne the expenses. Nor did Philip receive any satisfaction in the demand for Drake's punishment. For the next four or five years the great sailor remained ashore, serving, in 1582, as mayor of Plymouth, but all the while busying himself with matters connected with the sea.

Men like Drake were indeed, at this period, of the utmost value to England : the quarrel with Spain was growing keener, and Elizabeth, with all her skill, found it more and more difficult to keep the peace. Philip was almost absolute in Western Europe, and on the mainland only the people of the Netherlands opposed his power. They, with that stubborn bravery which has always marked them, were fighting his soldiers resolutely for every foot of their ground, and Elizabeth determined to aid them.

Philip replied by seizing all the English ships, goods, and men then in his dominions ; whereupon the Queen granted her subjects who had suffered by this, the right to pay themselves back by preying on the Spanish ships and settlements in the West Indies. And, still without declaring war, she resolved upon a bold measure. She herself would fit out a fleet of twenty-five vessels with which to strike a blow against Spain !

For such an enterprise the only possible leader was Sir Francis Drake, who, by his last feat, had so signally proved his ability and courage. As soon as the project became known, there was no lack of volunteers eager and anxious to serve under the great captain. Sir Philip Sidney, the Queen's chief favourite—who was afterwards slain in the Netherlands—arranged to sail with the expedition and went aboard for that purpose, but at the last moment an order from Elizabeth compelled him to return to London.

Besides the sailors, two thousand soldiers embarked at Plymouth, and these were under the command of Lieutenant-General Carleill, who was responsible for the military portion of the expedition. Drake was the general or admiral, while his vice-admiral was that stout-hearted Martin Frobisher, whose own name is one of the glories of the English navy.

By September 14, 1585, the preparations were complete, and on that date the expedition set forth from Plymouth, followed by the hopes and good wishes of the whole nation.

Drake steered a course for Vigo, where he captured several vessels containing valuable cargoes, and then ran across to Palma, in the Canary Islands; but, finding the Spaniards fully prepared to give him a warm reception, sailed to Porto Praya, in the West Indies, where he disembarked a thousand men, and foolishly, as events turned out, wasted some fourteen days. The governor of the place, and those who had anything to lose, fled to the mountains; but the rest remained, and one day, capturing an English boy who had strayed from his fellows, they put him to death with great cruelty. In revenge, Drake set fire to all the houses in the town of St. Jago and the neighbourhood.

This long stay at Porto Praya was productive of two evils: it gave the Spaniards in other places time to make ample preparations; and, owing either to the climate or food, such a terrible sickness broke out among the soldiers and sailors that nearly three hundred men died outright, while many more were so grievously afflicted that they never regained their former health and vigour.

From Porto Praya the expedition proceeded to the island of Dominica, inhabited at that time by the Caribs, a savage people—who, however, received the adventurers kindly, and assisted them in procuring fresh water for the fleet.

Christmas was spent at St. Christopher's, and then, after consulting with his officers, Drake decided to sail to the island of Hispaniola, and to capture the ancient and wealthy city of St. Domingo. The Spaniards had assembled in force; but Drake landed twelve hundred men about ten miles from the city, and placed them under the charge of Lieutenant-General Carleill, who divided his little army, giving one-half to Captain Powell.

The Spaniards had fortified both gates of the town, and had stationed men in ambush on the road: in addition, they sent out a small force of cavalry to drive the invaders back. But the two divisions pressed on, entered at both gates, drove the defenders from their positions, and fought their way by sheer strength to the square which is a feature of all Spanish cities. Here they fell to making trenches, and, having brought up their guns, entrenched themselves so strongly that they could not be dislodged, while they announced their intention of remaining there until the city was ransomed.

There was not much fighting, but one incident occurred which is worthy of mention. One day the general sent a negro boy, carrying a flag of truce, with a message to the governor. On his way he met a Spanish officer, who wounded him so severely, that the boy only just managed to crawl back to his master and relate the story before he died.

This was an outrage against all the laws of war, and the general inflicted a swift and deadly, though we can hardly call it a just, punishment. Among his prisoners were two friars, and these unhappy men he despatched with a guard of soldiers to the spot where the boy had been wounded. There they were both hanged, and at the same time a third prisoner was sent to the governor to say that, every day until the guilty officer was surrendered, two more prisoners should be put to death.

It was a stern and irregular proceeding, but it produced the desired effect. The officer was promptly delivered up, and the Spaniards were themselves compelled to execute him in the general's presence.

Meanwhile, the ransom demanded was not forthcoming, and, in order to quicken its payment, the sailors set fire every day to a portion of the outskirts of the city. But the houses were strongly built of stone, and the adventurers found their task so difficult, that every one was glad when the governor at length agreed to pay a ransom of five and twenty thousand ducats.

This business being concluded, preparations were made for continuing the voyage. The sailors helped themselves to a store of wine and other provisions, and some woollen and silk goods ; but of gold and silver, which was to them of chief value, they discovered little or none, as it had doubtless been securely hidden before their arrival.

CHAPTER VI.

"Singeing the King's Beard."

THUS far the expedition, from which so much had been expected, had not proved a brilliant success ; indeed, Drake had accomplished far more when he was in command of the *Golden Hind* alone. But Sir Francis and his rovers were not yet discouraged ; several fair towns remained to be captured, and the officers decided to strike a blow at Cartagena and Nombre de Dios in succession, and then, advancing overland to Panama, to seize the treasure which was being transported to Spain.

Standing over to the mainland, they entered the harbour of Cartagena, and found the town strongly fortified and barricaded against their advance ; but, nothing daunted by these obstacles, the landing party rushed at the walls, and, after a fierce hand-to-hand struggle, drove the Spaniards back and made themselves masters of the market-place. For six weeks they remained in possession, and, as the ransom demanded was not forthcoming, they set fire, first to one quarter of the town and then to another, until the inhabitants consented to the payment of one hundred and ten thousand ducats as ransom.

And here may be mentioned a very pleasing incident, which reveals the officers of the expedition in a most favourable light. Feeling that the men were endangering their lives and suffering severe hardships with but small benefit to themselves, the officers generally declared that—"What part or portion soever it be of this ransom for Cartagena, which should come unto us, we do freely give and bestow the same upon the men who have remained with us in the voyage, meaning as well the sailor as the soldier, and wishing with all our hearts it were such or so much, as might seem a sufficient reward for their endeavour."

The members of the expedition were by this time in a pitiful plight. The disease caught at the Cape Verde Islands had never left them; numbers died, and few of those attacked, even if they lived, were of much service afterwards. This deplorable state of affairs compelled Drake reluctantly to abandon the enterprise against Nombre de Dios, and to return home.

But the disasters which had hitherto dogged the expedition were not at an end. Finding no fresh water at Cape St. Antonis, in Cuba, they sailed for Matanzas; but a violent storm drove them back, and once more they landed near St. Antonis to resume the weary search. And here, through the records of one of the officers, we obtain a glimpse of Drake—cheering his men, looking after his ships, toiling hard and laboriously as if he had been but a common sailor, showing the greatness of his mind as much in these days of difficulty and gloom, as he had before done in the hours of his brightest success. This dreary expedition which resulted in failure, adds to, rather than detracts from, his fame.

Having, after tremendous labour, secured some rain-water, the adventurers set sail once more, and, coasting Florida, landed at two or three Spanish settlements, but without obtaining a great deal of booty, as the inhabitants wisely withdrew into the interior at the first sign of their approach. Continuing their voyage, they came at length to Sir Walter Raleigh's new colony of Virginia, which the Queen had commanded Sir Francis to visit.

The handful of colonists—there were only one hundred and three altogether—had suffered numerous hardships, and, as the promised supplies of provisions had failed to reach them, they begged to be taken back to England. Drake acceded to their request, and they were embarked on board his ships. To Mr. Lane, the governor of the colony, we probably owe the introduction of tobacco, a plant which he obtained from the island of Tobago. This embarkation of the disappointed colonists was the last event of any importance, the fleet arriving at Portsmouth in July 1586 — having lost no fewer than seven hundred and fifty men, almost all of whom had died of disease.

Drake, we may believe, was not particularly well pleased with the poor results of his voyage, and yet it had done excellent service in increasing the confidence of the English sailors in their own fighting powers. Wherever they had encountered the Spaniards they had beaten them easily, thus helping to dispel the fear with which the English were at that time accustomed to regard their formidable rivals.

And the need of this confidence was becoming more and more urgent. The hostility between England and Spain was growing so acute, that those at the head of affairs regarded a bitter and deadly war as inevitable. King Philip began to prepare for an invasion of England, hoping that the English Catholics would rise in his favour, and that by their aid he would be able to master the enemy. In this view, of course, he was mistaken; but there is little doubt that he counted largely on their assistance.

The secret of Philip's plans, however, was soon discovered by the English agents, and when he learned this, he threw off the mask, and boldly put forth a number of conditions, to which he demanded that Elizabeth should consent.

The most important of these were that Elizabeth should desert the cause of the Dutch; make ample amends for Drake's piracy; restore the monasteries destroyed by her father; and, finally, acknowledge the Pope as the head of the English Church.

Philip knew well that the English queen was

unlikely to comply with these requests, and his preparations for a decisive effort continued without ceasing. By this time all Europe recognised that he meant to crush his audacious rival, and there were few who did not believe that he would be able to do so.

But he and they reckoned without the hardy sailors who, under Drake and other leaders, had scoured the seas, had sacked the towns on the Spanish Main, had vanquished the Spaniards in nearly every engagement, and, most important of all, by constant practice had become the most skilful seamen in the world. The men of the seaport towns had matched themselves against the Spaniards, and had no misgivings as to the result of any encounter either on sea or land.

And now Elizabeth proved that she was not wanting in those qualities which we expect the ruler of this country to possess. By skill and craft, by cunning and even by double dealing, she had long warded off the evil ; she had striven hard for peace, but, now that war was in sight, she acted promptly and struck boldly.

To deliver the blow, an able and fearless sailor was required, and without hesitation she sent for Drake. The old rover was ready and willing to risk his life in any perilous adventure, and he did not pause to count the odds. And the task that the Queen set him must have made his heart leap for joy. He was to lead a fleet to Spain and discover just what Philip was doing— a very important undertaking.

But this was not all. In the Low Countries,

Philip's general was the Duke of Parma, and it was part of Drake's duties to capture all supplies of men and stores that were being conveyed to him. He was also to seize all the Spanish vessels he found at sea or in harbour, and to plunder them of their contents. This was a business after Drake's own heart, and he gladly accepted the commission.

The Queen gave him four of her best ships— the *Elizabeth Bonaventure, Lyon, Rainbow,* and *Dreadnought,* and the merchants of London supplied twenty others. The action of these merchants was a striking testimony to the confidence and trust which the nation placed in the leader of the expedition. They risked their ships and put their money into the venture, feeling certain that under Drake's command it would yield a rich interest.

Early in April 1587, the admiral had collected his squadron at Plymouth; and that he himself felt no misgiving as to the issue of the enterprise, may be gathered from his letter to Sir Francis Walsingham, in which he writes :—

"If your Honour did now see the fleet under sail, and knew with what resolution men's minds do enter into this action, that your Honour would rejoice to see them, so you would judge a small force would not divide them."

Confident of success, the squadron sailed from Plymouth on an enterprise which, from the skill and daring with which it was carried through, and from the results achieved, must ever remain memorable in our history.

During the voyage Drake fell in with two ships that had come from Cadiz, and learned from their masters that the harbour was crowded with vessels, busily taking in provisions and all kinds of warlike stores. This was pleasant news to the admiral, who did not doubt that, if he could arrive in time, the whole of the shipping would be at his mercy; and accordingly, with all sails set, he steered his course for Cadiz harbour.

To the joy of every one on board, the harbour was seen, when the English squadron ran into Cadiz roads, to be still filled with a crowd of shipping—defended by the guns of the castle, by several guardships, and by a number of powerful galleys. The enemy's strength might have made many a commander pause, but Drake did not hesitate for a moment. His prey was in front of him, and he resolved to go in and seize it. His men were as fearless as himself, and equally keen to deal the Spaniards a swift and crushing blow.

What follows reads almost like a romance. The rovers dashed at the entrance, sank the guardships, received the fire from the fortress without hurt, and attacked the galleys with such fury that, after a short but desperate combat, they were glad to retire under the shelter of the guns. All the small Spanish vessels that could pass the shoals fled into Porto Real, and the assailants were left masters of the harbour.

Then was witnessed a strange scene. The English sailors toiled unceasingly to transfer a large portion of the provisions to their own

vessels, and to sink or burn the Spanish ships.
In vain the guns of the fortress thundered; in
vain the galleys, considered by the Spaniards to
be more than a match for any English vessel
afloat, ventured from their shelter and fired
broadside after broadside at the destroyers—the
sailors continued their deadly work.

One after another the Spanish ships, large and
small, went to the bottom, or, enveloped in flames,
drifted seawards to be reduced in a short time
to charred hulks. And at length, in despair,
the Spaniards themselves aided in the work of
destruction. Unable to defend their vessels they
set them on fire, and turned them adrift in the
hope that they would set the English squadron
ablaze; but by incredible labour the sailors
managed to keep their vessels clear of the
burning craft.

For thirty-six hours the strange work continued,
until Drake had transferred sufficient provisions
and wine to last his whole armament for months,
and had utterly destroyed between thirty and forty
large vessels, besides numerous small ones. As
soon as the destruction was complete Drake steered
his ships out of the roads, having lost but very few
men in this memorable enterprise.

The cool audacity of the English admiral
astounded the Spaniards, who seemed dazed by
his proceedings; and their chief, the Marquis of
Santa Cruz, an able officer and distinguished
sailor, was so upset by the insult to his royal
master's flag, that he died within a few months,
leaving a vacant post which Philip found difficult

to fill. As for Drake, he sailed away in triumph, having, as he graphically expressed it, "singed the King of Spain's beard."

CHAPTER VII.

The Muttering of the Tempest.

WHAT Drake had witnessed in Cadiz harbour made it plain to him that Philip was straining every nerve to bring his plans to a successful issue, and we find the observant seaman writing home that "the like preparation was never heard of, nor known, as the King of Spain hath, and daily maketh to invade England. He is allied with mighty princes and dukes in the Straits, and his provisions of bread and wine are so great as will suffice 40,000 men a whole year."

But, although Drake recognised the extent of the danger, he was not in the least discouraged by it. "Our intention, therefore, is," he writes, "by God's help to intercept their meetings by all possible means we may;" and accordingly, as soon as the business at Cadiz was concluded, he steered towards Cape Sagres, sweeping the sea of every Spanish barque afloat, landing the crews, but burning the vessels with their stores intended for the invasion of England.

On arriving at Cape Sagres he found the harbour commanded by a castle and three fortresses, and, in order that his crews might not be annoyed by the heavy guns, he landed and stormed the castle, which, together with the forts, surrendered.

From Cape Sagres the squadron proceeded to Lisbon, where fifty galleons lay at anchor, and the intrepid English admiral was sorely tempted to make a dash for so rich a prize. However, he remained off the coast, scouring the seas, chasing every Spanish ship that appeared, burning and plundering, and doing a great deal of damage, without a single attempt being made to drive him from his cruising grounds.

In a letter to Sir Francis Walsingham, at this time, he writes: "As long as it shall please God to give us provisions to eat and drink, and that our ships and wind and weather will permit us, you shall surely hear of us near this Cape of St. Vincent." He does not appear to have taken into his head the possibility that the Spaniards would sally forth from Lisbon harbour and endeavour to crush him by sheer weight of ships and guns.

At last, having destroyed every craft foolish or unlucky enough to come within his reach, he sailed for the Azores, and his good fortune continued to accompany him. Near the island of St. Michael he encountered a Portuguese carrack, named the *Saint Philip,* which was on her homeward voyage from the East Indies. The carrack, unable to escape by flight, was speedily captured, with her costly and valuable cargo. The passengers and crew were transferred to some of the merchant vessels and allowed to depart in safety, and Drake, urged by his captains, consented to return to England.

This unexpected prize proved of extraordinary

value, and formed such a rich booty that, after
deducting the Queen's expenses—no inconsider-
able amount—enough remained to pay the various
London merchants a good interest for their share
in the hazardous venture to Cadiz.

This remarkable exploit, and the success with
which it had been executed, raised Drake's fame
higher than it had been before; and even those
people who had condemned his previous acts as
sheer piracy, could not withhold applause from
the man who had now rendered his country such
a striking service.

On this occasion he had sailed at the Queen's
express command, and, although war between
Spain and England had not been declared,
every one was aware it would be delayed only
until Philip was ready. For whatever faults the
King of Spain had, he was no weathercock to veer
with every changing gust of wind. He knew his
own mind; he knew what he wanted to do, and
he was resolved that it should be done.

England had thwarted him at every turn: her
soldiers had opposed him in the Low Countries;
her sailors had plundered his vessels on every sea.
But for English aid he believed the Dutch would
be at his feet, and that he would have stamped
Protestantism out of Holland. He felt, too, that
Elizabeth had tricked him, and he desired to
punish her. It is also possible he foresaw
dimly, that, unless England was crushed now,
she would usurp the proud position of Spain
among the nations.

Drake's "singeing" had done him immense

harm. He had lost men and ships and stores, and, until these were replaced, he could not deliver his attack. But, with a patience and a dogged obstinacy we cannot but admire, he endeavoured to make good the damage. Day and night, week in and week out, the work went steadily forward. Fresh stores were collected, more men enrolled, new ships built, and all the country resounded with the din of preparation.

But even while he laboured so strenuously, Philip lost that which could not be replaced. The Marquis of Santa Cruz, as we have before mentioned, died of grief, and the mighty armament was left without a head. The Spanish admiral was a splendid sailor, a stout-hearted fighting-man, and a leader trusted by every soldier and sailor who had served under him. Spain could better have afforded to lose half her fleet than Santa Cruz.

But no calamity could turn Philip from his fixed purpose. He called on the Duke of Medina Sidonia to take the place of the dead commander, and the duke, who was ignorant of sea-fighting, unwillingly obeyed. Philip appealed to his people for help, and—we must not lose sight of the fact—they responded nobly. Like their master, they half understood the truth that, for Spain to retain her power and influence, England must be crushed. They poured money with lavish hands into the king's coffers; they enrolled themselves with enthusiasm among the members of the expedition. They were our enemies, and they failed; but these things must not blind us to the truth.

Meanwhile, all Europe looked forward in wondering expectation. What would England do? What could England do against such a formidable opponent? For it must be understood that Philip was not relying for the success of his scheme wholly upon his Armada.

Alexander, Prince of Parma, the most noted general in Europe, was at the head of a large army in Flanders, and, while Philip was getting ready in Spain, Parma was doing his share in Flanders. With feverish activity he pushed on the building of flat-bottomed boats, sufficient to carry a hundred thousand men; he gathered together a vast supply of heavy guns, and implements for siege purposes, and he collected materials for bridge and fort building, and for forming camps. The Spanish fleet was to escort him to England, and, once landed, Parma felt confident of his ability to subdue the country. So, like a prudent and skilful general, he formed his plans, and saw that everything was in readiness for the time of striking the decisive blow.

It is not strange that the nations, knowing these things, thought England's knell had sounded; for how could one imagine that a poor and struggling country, as England then was, could hold her own against so fierce an attack?

But now was seen the value of the previous expeditions led by Drake, Hawkins, Frobisher, and a host of other daring and valiant captains. No one who had been out with Drake feared the result of a tussle with the Spaniards. Drake had captured too many Spanish vessels, and had fought successfully against long odds on too many occasions, to be afraid now, and he imparted his own courage to his men.

Then, again, the English sailors were masters of their profession, which meant much. In their small vessels they had braved every danger of the ocean : they had been scorched in the tropics, and frozen in the icy north ; they had been half-starved for want of provisions, and they had nearly perished of thirst ; without charts, they had steered their course across unknown seas ; they had been tossed like corks from crest to depth of mountainous waves ; they had scudded under bare poles before the wildest hurricanes, and had beaten home in the teeth of the most furious gales : neither Spaniard nor storm had for them the slightest terror.

It has already been said that Philip counted largely on the support of the English Roman Catholics, and, while he was preparing for the invasion, frequent messages were despatched by his numerous spies, which had the effect of confirming his opinion. But in this he made a grievous mistake : the Catholics did not forget they were Englishmen, and they placed themselves shoulder to shoulder with their Protestant brethren. The whole country was astir, and the warlike action of Elizabeth inflamed the zeal and patriotism of her people.

Collecting an army at Tilbury Fort, in order to bar the approach to the capital, she addressed her soldiers in a striking and memorable speech which did honour to herself and her kingdom.

She had been advised by some of her counsellors

to beware of treachery, but, addressing her soldiers, she exclaimed : " Let tyrants fear : I have always so behaved myself, that, under God, I have placed my chiefest strength and safeguard in the loyal hearts and goodwill of my subjects. And therefore I have come amongst you at this time, to live or die amongst you all ; to lay down, for my God, and for my kingdom, and for my people, my honour and my blood, even in the dust. I know I have but the body of a weak and feeble woman, but I have the heart of a king, and of a King of England, too. I myself will be your general, judge, and rewarder of every one of your virtues in the field."

But it was not in her soldiers, brave as they were, that England put her chief trust. Then, as now, the navy was the first line of defence, and it was to the navy that the guarding of the kingdom was really committed. Elizabeth, who, as a rule, kept a watchful guard over her purse-strings, realised that the life of the country was bound up in the struggle, and she resolved to strain every nerve to emerge victorious.

For some years the care of the navy had been committed to Sir John Hawkins, who turned out his vessels in fit condition ; but there were only thirty-four ships altogether, the largest of which was the *Triumph,* of 1100 tons, commanded by Sir Martin Frobisher. But the navy was not left to fight the battle alone. Every port in the kingdom contributed to the defence, and many a rough sea-rover who had sailed the Spanish seas gladly hastened to place his weather-beaten.

craft at the Queen's disposal. Mere cockle-shells some of them were compared with the Spanish galleons, but the men on board were experienced sailors and fearless fighters. Well was it for England, in the hour of her need, that she had bred such a strong and virile race.

Meanwhile, it may be asked, "What of Sir Francis Drake?" On his return from the expedition to Cadiz, he had employed his leisure in a work which the good folk of Plymouth recall with pride to this day. At that time the citizens possessed no water, and were compelled to fetch all they required from the distance of a mile. To Drake's genius, activity, and liberality they owed the bringing of a clear, pure stream to the very head of the town—a tedious and difficult undertaking which would not have been begun but for the patriotism of our hero.

The old sea-rover, however, had scant leisure for these peaceful pursuits ; his country needed his services, and it was with a joyful heart he obeyed the summons of Elizabeth to proceed to London. Charles, Lord Howard of Effingham, the Lord High Admiral of England, had been appointed to the chief command, and Drake, the finest sailor that England had yet produced, was selected by Elizabeth as Vice-Admiral and second in command—a proud position for one who, by his own merits, had risen from the humblest ranks. Prompt and resolute as ever, Drake, directly after his appointment, hurried back to Plymouth and hoisted his flag on the *Revenge*.

CHAPTER VIII.

The Storm Breaks.

IT is not surprising to read that, as soon as Drake had gone aboard the *Revenge,* he was anxious to strike a blow against the enemy ; nor that, in his opinion, a swift and sudden attack was the surest means of defence.

"My very good Lords," he writes to the Queen's advisers, "the advantage of time and place will be the only and chief means for our good. With fifty sail we shall do more good upon their own coast, than a great many more will do here at home, and the sooner we are gone the better."

And again, to Elizabeth herself he writes : "The advantage of time and place in all martial actions is half a victory, which, being lost, is irrecoverable ; wherefore if your Majesty will command me away with those ships that are here already, and the rest to follow with all possible expedition, I hold it in my poor opinion the surest and best course."

This letter was written on April 13, 1588, and on the 28th of April, so full was he of his subject, we find him sending a third letter, in which he says : "These great preparations for the Spaniards may be prevented by sending your forces to encounter them somewhat far off, and more near their own coast, which will be the better cheap for your Majesty and people, and much the dearer for the enemy."

On the 23rd of May, Lord Howard arrived at Plymouth, where he found Drake ready with sixty ships, and, no doubt by the advice of Sir Francis, he immediately put to sea and sailed to within a short distance of Spain, when a strong wind drove him back to Plymouth.

But the Queen's advisers were not willing that the English coasts should be left unprotected, and the admiral was instructed not to go so far away —an order which, of necessity, he was forced to obey, and the whole fleet was kept henceforth snug in Plymouth harbour.

Meanwhile, the Spaniards, full of zeal and enthusiasm, and having no doubt as to the success of the expedition, were burning with ardour to begin the crusade. From the lowest to the highest all alike were anxious to meet the enemy, and it is recorded that there was not a noble family in the land who had not one or more representatives on board the stately galleons.

Religion, too, was pressed into the service. Twelve of the ships were named after the Twelve Apostles; the monks animated the soldiers and sailors; the Pope gave his encouragement to the cause; and the Spaniards felt they were about to do battle not only for the honour of their country, but also for the success of their religion.

Drake had committed immense havoc at Cadiz, but that was an incident which they easily explained away; and, indeed, when one remembers their resources, it is not hard to understand why they felt so certain of gaining a decisive and overwhelming victory.

Their ships were fewer than those of the English, but in every other respect they had twice the force. There were, altogether, one hundred and thirty-two vessels, manned by nearly 9000 sailors and 2000 galley-slaves; while, in addition, some 20,000 soldiers were on board. The large vessels, with their high forecastles and lofty poops, resembled floating castles rather than ships, and served as forts from which the soldiers could sweep down with volleys of musketry any number of boarders who tried to clamber on to the main deck.

In addition to these castled vessels were massive galleons, serviceable galiasses, and a fleet of hulks containing stores of ammunition and provisions. The failure of the Armada does not rest on Philip's shoulders, as he had done everything in his power to insure success. In laying down his plan of operations, however, the Spanish monarch was misled by false information, and a similar cause afterwards led the commanders of the expedition into further error.

The Duke of Medina Sidonia received instructions to keep as near to the French coast as possible, to avoid the English fleet, and to proceed to Calais. Here it was arranged that he should be met by the Duke of Parma with his flat-bottomed boats and 40,000 soldiers. If Parma had not arrived, the fleet was to seek safe anchorage and await his coming; then the combined forces were to cross the Channel, enter the Thames, and capture London.

Evidently, in drawing up this scheme, Philip

did not take into account that Lord Henry
Seymour, with sixty Dutch and English vessels,
was keeping Parma closely shut up in harbour.
He must also have formed a very poor opinion
of the English leaders, if he really imagined
they would stand idly by while the Armada
wrought the ruin of their country.

As it chanced, however, Philip's plan was not
carried out.   The Armada departed from the
Tagus amidst the ringing cheers of assembled
thousands, who thought that already England
was as good as conquered.   But the triumphal
start received a disheartening check.   A terrific
storm arose, dismasted several of the vessels, and
sent them all scudding into the Groyne.

And now those in command acted upon a
second false piece of information.   The master
of an English ship, when questioned, declared
that the English fleet was lying quietly in
Plymouth Sound, and not at all in a condition
to oppose the Armada.

You will remember that the chief of the expedition was Medina Sidonia ; but he had little
experience of naval warfare, and he relied very
properly on the advice of Don Diego de Florez,
one of the ablest sailors in the Spanish navy.
On hearing the report of the English mariner,
Florez promptly proposed to sail to Plymouth
and destroy the English fleet, arguing that the
country would then lie at their mercy.   This was
capital advice, and the duke cannot be blamed
for accepting it.

Two centuries later, the most famous admiral

of all times adopted the same course. "Seek the enemy's fleet and destroy it," was Nelson's motto, and, had he led the Spanish Armada, he would probably have done the same thing that Florez counselled. With their huge fleet victory was almost a foregone conclusion, and then the Spaniards could have landed their troops and established themselves at almost any point on the coast they cared to select. The Duke of Sidonia agreed with his adviser, and the Armada once again set sail, this time heading straight for Plymouth Sound.

Meanwhile, the English fleet was lying in the harbour, but fully prepared to do battle with the enemy as soon as they appeared in sight. Swift barques cruised in the Channel, keeping a sharp lookout for the foe, while the sailors waited at their posts for the moment of action.

At Plymouth are two natural harbours, between which stretches a bold ridge known as Plymouth Hoe, from which a fine view can be obtained of the Channel. Here, one afternoon in July 1588, were assembled the principal commanders of the English fleet, among them being Lord Howard, Drake, Hawkins, Frobisher, and Raleigh. According to tradition, they were passing the time by playing at bowls, one of the oldest English games.

That the following story is true cannot be affirmed, but it has become one of the traditions of our history, and there must be few British boys to whom it is unknown. In the middle of the game, according to one version, a small pinnace was observed evidently in a great hurry, and making the best of her way into the harbour. The master of the pinnace, one Fleming, a pirate, landed in hot haste with the information that he had that morning sighted the Spanish fleet off the Cornish coast.

From man to man the startling report ran ; the sailors on shore hastened to their ships, and the captains were about to abandon their sport, when Drake firmly insisted that the game should be played out. "For," he observed calmly, "there will be plenty of time to finish the game and to beat the Spaniards too."

The story may be incorrect, but it would not be a matter of surprise if Drake really behaved in this manner in order to keep his comrades from over-rating the danger. But, in any case, the delay must have been short, for there was much to be done. It was necessary to tow the ships out of the port, and we are told that the wind was blowing stiffly into the harbour, making the operation both tedious and dangerous.

On the following day, July 20, 1588, the Armada was observed advancing slowly up the Channel, the huge ships with their massive turrets, their sails set, and the whole fleet, in the shape of a half-moon, forming a magnificent picture. On the 21st of July, the first shot in the memorable contest was fired by a little pinnace called the *Disdain,* which Lord Howard sent out as a challenge to the enemy. Then like the brave and gallant nobleman he was, the admiral dashed into the fight with his own

S.D.

"Plenty of time to finish the game."

flagship, the *Ark Royal,* and "thundered thick and furiously upon a large ship which he thought to be the Spanish admiral, but was that of Alphonso de Leyva."

And, while Lord Howard was thus battling with his formidable opponent, Drake, Hawkins, and Frobisher were as stoutly assailing the rear. Their vessels were so handy—sailing two feet to one of the enemy—and the sailors were so skilful, that they did almost as they pleased. And the gunners were equally masters of their profession. The huge balls of the Spaniards, fired slowly, passed high and harmlessly over the English craft, whereas the galleons offered such splendid targets that almost every discharge from our guns took effect.

General Juan de Recalde commanded the Spanish rear, and he and his men were bewildered by the activity of their foe. They could do nothing; their ships moved slowly, and could not be easily turned, while the English ran in closely, delivered their fire, and passed on to another hostile vessel. The general's ship appears to have been tremendously battered; her rigging was cut up and her foremast disabled. Others were in nearly as bad condition, and the Duke of Medina Sidonia, perceiving the plight of his comrades, took in his sails and waited for the stragglers to close up.

For two hours the fight continued, and then Lord Howard stopped the pursuit, as the last of his ships to leave Plymouth harbour had not yet joined. Drake was not much impressed by this first day's action, as we find him writing to Lord Seymour: "The army of Spain arrived upon our coast the 20th of this month: the 21st we had them in chase; and on coming up unto them there hath passed some common shot between some of our fleet and some of theirs; and, as far as we perceive, they are determined to sell their lives with blows."

In a message to the Duke of Parma some days afterwards, the Spanish admiral says: "The enemy pursue me; they fire upon me most days from morning to night, but they will not close and grapple, and there is no remedy, for they are swift and we are slow." This, indeed, was the secret of the English success, and we must not imagine that the Spaniards were not ready and willing to wage a stout-hearted fight if they could but have come to hand-grips.

However, the dreaded Armada had made its appearance, and the result of the first brief contest was to put heart into our men and to show them that they were a match, and more than a match, for the far-famed Spanish Dons. But, although Lord Howard had thus scored a distinct success, he was not without his troubles. At the moment of victory he writes to Sir F. Walsingham in this strain: "Sir, for the love of God and our country, let us have with some speed some great shot sent us of all bigness, for this service will continue long; and some powder with it."

Even in the crisis of our country's fortunes, when a defeat of the navy would have involved the total ruin of Elizabeth's power, the Queen continued to keep tight hold of the purse-strings, and to provide the captains of her ships with the smallest possible amount of supplies.

CHAPTER IX.

Fire, Storm, and Ruin.

MISFORTUNE still continued to dog the course of the Armada. That very evening one of their largest flagships took fire, purposely kindled, it is recorded in some accounts, by a Dutch gunner who had received some ill-usage from his Spanish masters. Whether this story be true or not, it is certain that a quantity of gunpowder exploded and blew up the two decks and the poop, besides injuring a number of the crew. By the aid of the nearest Spanish ships the fire was got under, and, for a time, the vessel was saved.

Shortly afterwards a disaster, which had even more serious results, occurred. The galleon commanded by Don Pedro de Valdez, one of the most experienced of the Spanish leaders, fell foul of another vessel, and was so disabled that she could not keep up with the rest of the fleet. Here was a puzzle for the Duke of Medina Sidonia to solve. What should he do? His van was already some distance ahead, and, if he waited for his comrade, morning would find the Armada in two widely separated divisions.

Don Diego de Florez advised pushing on. It

was folly, he urged, to hazard the success of the expedition for the object of rescuing a single ship, and the Duke, adopting this view, abandoned Valdez to his fate. The disabled galleon, rolling helplessly in the heavy seas, lagged farther and farther behind, and in the morning was spied by Drake, who instantly sent his pinnace to demand her surrender.

Valdez endeavoured to make terms, but the Englishman replied he had no leisure for parley, and that unless the galleon promptly struck her flag he would send her to the bottom. As soon as the Spaniards discovered who their antagonist was, they gave up the ship, which was sent into Dartmouth, but not before Drake had rifled her of the treasure on board, which amounted to 35,000 ducats in gold. This desertion of Don Pedro still further depressed the Spaniards, and must be regarded as a great mistake on the part of the duke.

But that same night Drake himself, led away by over-zeal, committed a grave error of judgment. His vessel, the *Revenge*—apt name for the rover's craft — carried the light which was a signal to the other ships; but Drake, observing some strange vessels, started off in pursuit. The rest of his squadron, losing sight of the signal, remained behind; but Lord Howard, following the light of a Spanish galleon, which he mistook for Drake's, discovered himself at dawn in the midst of the enemy's fleet. Fortunately he managed to slip away in time, and no harm resulted; but the incident might have ended far otherwise.

That day the battle was maintained with the utmost fury and amid great confusion. Here a number of merchant ships, surrounded by Spaniards, were rescued by Lord Howard; while in the rear the Spaniards fought with the most stubborn courage to beat off Drake's attack on the squadron of Recalde. Again and again the Dons endeavoured to board; but this was impossible, owing to the lightness of the English ships and the wonderful skill with which they were navigated.

Some of the English captains, burning to finish the contest, advised the admiral to issue orders for boarding in his turn; but this he very wisely declined to do. It paid him much better to maintain a running fight, to harass the enemy as much as possible, and to preserve his own vessels from destruction. England had only the one fleet, and, if that were destroyed, the enemy would be free to land at their pleasure.

The next day passed without fighting, and the admiral seized the opportunity to send some of his smaller vessels to the neighbouring ports for a supply of powder and shot: he also divided his fleet into four squadrons, commanding one himself, and placing the three others under the charge of Drake, Hawkins, and Frobisher.

On the 25th of July, the Armada, still hotly pursued by the English, had reached the Isle of Wight, and urgent messages were despatched to the Duke of Parma that he would come swiftly with assistance. But the duke either could not, or would not move, and the Armada, proceeding on its course, anchored off Calais. Lord Howard, joined by Lord Seymour's division, anchored not far off, and waited for the next move.

Thus far the Armada remained undefeated; indeed, so tremendous was its strength that the losses it had met with might almost be disregarded. The duke had done what was required of him; he had brought his ships to Calais roads, and, if Parma would only do his part, all might yet go well. Still Parma remained inactive, and, while the Spanish leaders deliberated, Lord Howard decided on a plan which was to cause them serious mischief.

Selecting eight of the worst ships, he filled them with pitch, resin, and a host of inflammable materials; loaded all their guns with chain-shot, and placed them under the command of two daring seamen—Captains Young and Prowse. Then shortly after midnight, with the wind and tide behind them, he sent the destructive flotilla straight for the Spanish fleet.

Suddenly the darkness of the night was dispelled by a tremendous blaze, and the enemy, awakened from sleep, beheld the dreaded fireships drifting into the midst of their crowded galleons. The Duke of Sidonia had made arrangements to defeat this plan, and had given orders that on the approach of the fireships his galleons should weigh anchor and resume their station when the danger was over.

But the broad sheets of flame, the roar of the bursting guns, the hurtling of the shot, proved too much for the enemy's nerves. A startled cry of fear and terror rang out on the night air. "Cut the cables!" yelled the sailors; "cut the cables!" and instantly all was confusion and chaos. Every vessel that could, stood out to sea; but some were disabled, and one, rudderless and unmanageable, was driven on the sands before Calais. Here she was observed at daylight by Howard, who dashed at her with his boats, over-whelmed the soldiers and sailors, set the galley-slaves free, and rifled the stranded vessel of fifty thousand gold ducats.

Meanwhile, Drake was addressing himself to more serious work. The Spaniards were drifting along the coast in confusion, and Drake led his squadron straight at them. He was in his element now, and the captains of his ships emulated his zeal. The Spaniards were at a terrible disadvan-tage; at every point they were out-classed by their light and active opponents.

But they could die valiantly for the honour of their country, and this they did in hundreds. With falling masts and wrecked rigging, with guns dismantled and decks strewn with the dying and dead, they fought on, hopelessly, but with unsubdued spirit. Private soldiers, hot-blooded young nobles, veteran hidalgos of the bluest blood in Spain stayed at their posts until released by death. Whenever a galleon, riddled by shot, lagged behind, there flew the English ships pouring broadside after broadside into their unhappy foe. Some were captured, some sunk, others were driven ashore sheer hulks, while the whole mighty fleet was scattered over the face of the waters. But men and leaders, after the first panic, behaved nobly, and haughty Spain had no reason to be ashamed of the conduct of her sons that dreadful day.

The main body of the fleet drifted toward the shoals of Zealand, and every vessel must have been wrecked but for a sudden change of wind which enabled them to steer their course northward. Then the duke, calling his officers together, held a hurried council, and it was decided that they should go back to the Channel. But the contrary wind rendered this impossible, and finally they concluded to return home by way of the North Sea.

The expedition had failed in its object; the men were worn out by fighting and hard toil; disease had made its appearance, most of the ammunition had been expended, and provisions were scarce. The Spaniards were, indeed, in evil case, and their opponents were not much better off. They had little ammunition left, while fever and scurvy were striking the sailors down by scores. Yet they continued the chase, being uncertain what course the beaten foe would follow.

Drake's opinion is clearly shown in one of his letters to the Queen. "If the wind hinder it not, I think they are forced to Denmark; and that for divers causes: certain it is that many of their people were sick, and not a few killed. Their ships, sails, and ropes needeth great reparations, for that they had all felt of your Majesty's force. If your Majesty thought it meet, it were not amiss you sent to Denmark to understand the truth, and to deal with their king according to your Majesty's great wisdom."

It is apparent, too, that he felt rather uneasy concerning the doings of Parma, for in another letter he writes: "The Prince of Parma, I take him to be as a bear robbed of her whelps; and, no doubt, being so great a soldier as he is, that he will presently, if he may, undertake some great matter."

This very natural anxiety was, however, without cause: Parma attempted nothing, and the Spaniards were utterly helpless. Howard and Drake followed them as far as the Firth of Forth, and then, having taken in a fresh store of provisions, turned back, leaving the Armada to make the best of its way home round the north of Scotland and the west coast of Ireland.

The story of that terrible voyage has often been told. A fearful storm scattered the fleet; ship after ship was cast ashore or engulfed in the raging waters; men died in scores through weakness and disease, and disaster followed upon disaster until the Armada was reduced to a pitiful wreck of its former self.

The loss inflicted by the English was as nothing compared with that caused by the elements. And of help or means of safety there was none this side of Spain. So, stricken with fever and scurvy, the poor mariners toiled on, navigating their battered hulks as best they could. The line of galleons became less as the vessels ploughed their path round the north of Scotland, and along the west coast of Ireland.

Here, in the black night, in the midst of a howling tempest, one was engulfed in the raging waters, and all on board perished, their fate only guessed at by their surviving comrades. There, another, rudderless and altogether unmanageable, was dashed against the iron-bound coast, where those of the crew who escaped death by drowning died of starvation or were captured by the soldiers.

It is said by the old historians that only fifty-three battered hulks of all the splendid Armada reached Spain — eighty-one ships and nearly fourteen thousand men having been lost in the expedition. The shock was a severe one to Philip, who had reckoned so confidently on success; but it did not break his iron will. Signs of mourning were displayed by almost every family in Spain, while there was not a single noble house that did not count one or more of its members among the victims.

The Duke of Medina Sidonia, who had not wished to lead the fleet, returned home a broken old man; while another of those high in command was carried to his bed, where, turning his face to the wall, he died broken-hearted.

In England the rejoicings were universal; and every Protestant nation in Europe joined in the general chorus of thanksgiving at the destruction of the formidable fleet. A day was selected for a public service to be held at St. Paul's, where all the trophies captured from the enemy were placed, after having been carried in a triumphal procession. Lord Howard and his officers were rewarded

by their grateful sovereign ; nor were the services
of the seamen forgotten.

Several medals were struck in honour of the
decisive victory—one which represented a flying
fleet had the words, *Venit, Vidit, Fugit* inscribed.
Another pointed to the belief, very general at the
time, that Elizabeth herself suggested the use of
fireships at Calais. The medal represents several
vessels in flames bearing down on a crowded
fleet, while the inscription is *Dux Fœmina facti,*
though there is not any trustworthy evidence that
Lord Howard owed the origin of his successful
stratagem to his sovereign.

CHAPTER X.

To Portugal with Don Antonio.

THE destruction of the Armada, although it
lessened the peril to England, did not render
our land altogether secure from invasion.
Philip's grand attempt had failed, but he was far
from being the man to wring his hands over his
failure, and to abandon all his hopes in despair.
Failure was only an incentive to fresh efforts, and
it soon became known that he was busily employed
in collecting a fresh fleet. As a matter of fact, the
Spanish monarch was fully as obstinate as his
English rivals.

Remembering Drake's former advice, Elizabeth
now resolved to attack the Spaniards at home, or,
rather, in the country of Portugal, which had been
added to the Spanish dominions.

Now it chanced that there was in England a certain Don Antonio, a member of the royal family of Portugal, and he persuaded Elizabeth that, if she would support his claim to the throne, the Portuguese would rise in his favour and expel their Spanish masters from the country. An expedition was accordingly undertaken, with Sir John Norris as military chief, and Drake as commander of the fleet.

Unfortunately, the affair was badly managed. The Queen supplied six warships, but the remainder of the fleet belonged to private adventurers. A long delay, too, occurred, as the vessels lay a whole month at Plymouth, detained by contrary winds.

All this time the soldiers and sailors required to be fed, and Elizabeth, as usual, was exceedingly sparing of her money. Drake and Norris provided what they could out of their own private fortunes, until their resources were exhausted; and we find Drake writing bitterly to Lord Burleigh, begging for fresh supplies. The soldiers also were ill-found in arms and ammunition, and only the most hopeful of men could have looked forward to the success of the enterprise.

However, the expedition put to sea, when a violent storm dispersed the fleet, and twenty-five ships, carrying 3,000 men, returned to England. The main body sailed on to the Groyne—that is, the Bay of Corunna—where the vessels cast anchor. The next day the soldiers attacked the lower part of the town, which they carried after a short but sharp fight, and, having secured a large amount of oil and wine for their own use, the invaders destroyed the remainder, together with a quantity of stores and provisions collected for the next expedition to England.

Several ships of war found in the harbour were captured and burned, while the Spaniards themselves set fire to the *San Juan,* one of the largest galleons that had formed part of the Armada. For two days this vessel continued ablaze, until she was burned down to the water's edge.

Meanwhile, the attack on the upper town was stoutly resisted, but, the explosion of a mine having brought down half of a tower and made a breach in the walls, our men rushed to the assault. A lucky accident for the Spaniards occurred: the other half of the tower fell, and buried numbers of the assailants beneath its ruins. The assault failed, nor did the soldiers find better success at any other point.

Every advance was met with the utmost bravery by the defenders, who were encouraged by a woman, Maria Pita, the wife of an ensign. With sword and buckler she took her stand wherever the danger was greatest, preserving her courage even when her husband was slain before her eyes. As a reward for her brilliant services, Philip ordered that she should receive the full pay of an ensign from that time until her death.

Finally, General Norris was compelled to abandon his design, but, before embarking his troops, he had to fight a battle with a Spanish army of 17,000 men. Again the Spaniards offered a stout resistance, repulsing a first assault; but our men, nothing daunted, returned to the attack, and, in a short time, the enemy fled in all directions, abandoning their weapons and baggage to the victors. Still it was evident that the higher town could not be stormed; so, after having plundered and burned the neighbouring villages, the troops returned to their ships.

During the voyage along the coast of Portugal, the expedition was joined by the Earl of Essex, who, anxious to distinguish himself by some war-like deed, had secretly sailed from England without the Queen's permission. The hot-headed young nobleman soon had ample opportunity to prove his courage and daring. Forty miles or so from Lisbon is Peniche, and here it was decided to make a fresh descent. The surf ran high, but the troops landed, with the loss of some twenty men whose boat was overturned.

Led by Essex, the soldiers advanced, and, driving the Spaniards before them, entered the town. A stout resistance might have been offered by the garrison of the neighbouring castle, but the officer in command consented to surrender, and to acknowledge Don Antonio as the rightful king of Portugal.

Fired by this success, Sir John Norris determined on marching overland to Lisbon, being encouraged by the hope and belief that all the chief men of the country would flock to Don Antonio's standard. Drake, of course, remained in charge of the fleet, but he stayed on shore to witness the departure of the army. As the troops marched past, he took his leave of them and promised that, if the weather did not hinder, he would sail with his ships to the Portuguese capital.

Norris soon discovered that the support which Don Antonio had promised would not be forthcoming. A few peasants joined the invaders, but the nobility and gentry held sullenly aloof. But the English leader pressed forward, and, although many of his men suffered severely from the scorching heat, while others died for want of food, he arrived safe before the gates of Lisbon. Once or twice the Spaniards had endeavoured to bar his progress, but he had brushed aside their opposition with the utmost ease.

Now he occupied the suburbs of the town, treating the inhabitants with kindness, and forbidding his troops on pain of death to plunder or molest them in any way. But the Portuguese, either dreading the vengeance of the Spaniards or being perfectly indifferent to the claims of Don Antonio, refused to render any assistance, and Norris found himself in a difficult position.

He had advanced with a meagre army to the very gates of a large and strongly fortified city, expecting that Don Antonio's friends would afford him entrance, which they made no effort to do. Disease had made its appearance and his men were dying fast, while, strangely enough, he had not even a single field-piece with which to batter down one of the gates.

The soldiers had neither matches nor powder for their muskets, and were in no condition to meet the Spaniards who from time to time sallied forth from the town. But even thus, without ammunition, and weakened by disease and want of food, the troops retained their reputation for valour, and more than once, led by the fiery Essex, chased the enemy back to the gates. Indeed, so strongly did their resolution impress the garrison that Lisbon would have been surrendered if Sir John Norris had possessed but a single battery of artillery.

At length the general, recognising that the prize was beyond his reach, reluctantly decided to abandon the siege, and to march overland to Cascais, where Drake lay with his ships. The retreat caused the liveliest satisfaction among the Spaniards, and one of their leaders proclaimed that the English army had been routed and put to flight. This falsehood angered both Sir John and the Earl of Essex, the latter of whom sent the Spanish officer a letter challenging him to single combat, and proposing, if this offer did not suit him, that ten Englishmen should meet ten Spaniards on equal terms; but neither proposal was accepted.

At Cascais the soldiers, wearied and disease-ridden, found the ships of the expedition, and little time was wasted in embarking. And now we must turn our attention to Drake, to learn somewhat of his movements. When the army left Peniche on their march to Lisbon, Drake had promised to meet them there if the weather did not hinder him, and the admiral's enemies were quick to blame him for the failure of the ill-judged enterprise.

But it is not by any means certain that even had

Drake reached Lisbon, the disaster would have
been averted. The real cause of the ill-success
lay in the indifference of the Portuguese to Don
Antonio, and in the niggardliness with which the
expedition had been fitted out. Even at the start
the troops were short of provisions, and, in their
feeble state, caused chiefly by want of food, they
fell a ready prey to disease.

And but for the cruel death it brought to many
gallant men, it would be ludicrous to think of a
small army marching through a hostile country,
with not enough powder for the soldiers' muskets,
and sitting down before a fortified town without
a single cannon to point at the gates. Had
Sir John Norris been properly provided with
provisions and ammunition, there is no doubt that
he would have scored a signal success; though it
is extremely improbable that the Portuguese would
have accepted Don Antonio as their sovereign.

But while the army had wasted its strength
on shore, Drake had not been idle. On his
way to Cascais he had captured numerous ships
laden with naval stores for Lisbon, and others
designed as ships of war, all intended to form
part of a new armada. Entering the harbour at
Cascais, he seized sixty foreign vessels which
had arrived there with stores for the Spaniards,
and, in order that his men might not be molested
from the shore, he destroyed the castle and forced
the garrison to surrender.

Now, as soon as the soldiers were embarked,
the ships put to sea; but the series of misfortunes was not yet at an end—a wild storm

arose, and seventeen days passed before the fleet was able to reach Vigo. Meanwhile, men were dying daily of sickness and actual hunger, and at Vigo the leaders discovered they had not above two thousand men who were in a fit condition to carry arms.

But the position was so desperate that it was resolved to land and endeavour to secure a supply of provisions. The inhabitants, however, fled from the town, carrying off everything of value except a store of wine, of which the soldiers promptly took possession ; and then, having ravaged the district for several miles, they returned to their ships.

As it was impossible to do anything further on the Portuguese coast, Sir John Norris agreed that Drake should take the strongest men in twenty of the stoutest ships, and endeavour to intercept the Spanish treasure-fleet on its homeward voyage from America, while the rest returned to England.

Drake, unfortunately, missed the enemy and sailed for Plymouth, where Sir John Norris arrived some time afterwards, and the survivors of the expedition were disbanded. There was little rejoicing in England at the result of the enterprise, which had cost the lives of six thousand soldiers and sailors in sickness alone. But it must not be forgotten that the Spaniards had suffered much damage both in men and material, while the English soldiers had proved again that in open fight they were more than a match for their traditional foe.

After his return to England, Drake still continued active in his country's service both at sea and in Parliament, where he sat as the member for Plymouth. As might have been expected from a man of his character, he spoke earnestly in favour of making England strong by land and sea, and any warlike measure brought forward received his approval. But in 1593 the Parliament was dissolved, and the veteran sailor was called upon to take a prominent part in a new and hazardous venture. It was to be the last occasion on which he would lead an English fleet against the foe, and, unhappily, it was fated to end in disaster.

CHAPTER XI.

The Death of a Sea-King.

THE war with Spain still dragged on, and frequent expeditions were despatched to the Western seas in order to capture the Spanish treasure-ships. But Philip was a crafty as well as a sturdy foe, and so carefully did he lay his plans that the English adventurers met with scant success.

Lord Thomas Howard was foiled on that memorable occasion when Sir Richard Grenville fought his ship, the *Revenge*—Drake's old flagship — for twelve hours against a Spanish squadron ; Hawkins and Frobisher were equally unsuccessful, and for seven months did not capture a single prize. Now, Drake was to be placed in command of a squadron, and, in spite of the partial failure at Lisbon, every one looked forward to a triumphant voyage.

Elizabeth provided six ships from the Royal Navy, while, in addition, there were twenty others belonging to private persons. The commander of the troops was Sir Thomas Baskerville, while Drake had as vice-admiral his early friend and patron, Sir John Hawkins, now an old man at least seventy-five years of age and in feeble health. The main object of the expedition was to seize the treasure-ships supposed to be in harbour at Puerto Rico.

The expedition left Plymouth on August 28, 1595, and proceeded straight to the Grand Canary, which Drake and Baskerville decided to capture; though their veteran comrade spoke strongly against the proposal, urging that valuable time would be wasted and the Spaniards made aware of their design. Unable to land at the first selected spot on account of the surf, they proceeded to the western side of the island; but, one of their men being taken prisoner, the Spaniards learned from him the real object of the enterprise.

The next stop was at Guadaloupe, but the Spaniards had been put on the alert, and one of the vessels belonging to Sir John Hawkins's division was captured. This reverse is reported to have preyed on the spirits of the rugged old admiral; he was seized with a sudden illness, and in a short time breathed his last. It was a melancholy end to the career of a man who,

"A cannon-ball smashed the stool."

whatever his faults may have been, had done good work for England.

Sir Thomas Baskerville now took the place of the dead chief, and the squadron proceeded to Puerto Rico, where the vessels anchored. That same evening the adventurers received a foretaste of what was in store for them. While Drake, surrounded by several of his officers, sat at supper, a cannon-ball smashed the stool on which he was sitting and wounded two of his comrades so severely that they died. One was Brute Browne, an old and trusted friend of the admiral.

"Ah, dear Brute," exclaimed Drake, "I could grieve for thee! but now is no time for me to let down my spirits."

Drake, indeed, required all his skill and courage for the desperate enterprise upon which he was engaged. The enemy had learned of his coming, and were prepared. The treasure had been removed from the galleon, which was sunk in the mouth of the harbour, forming part of a barrier which rendered the entrance well nigh impassable, while the heavy guns of several forts commanded the waterway.

But, hazardous as was the attempt to force an entrance, the English sailors in their boats and pinnaces dashed to the attack with stout hearts. A raking fire met them; but they pressed on, and succeeded in destroying six vessels that lay in the harbour. The men, however, fell fast, until, with nearly fifty killed and as many wounded, the detachment of boats rejoined the main body. The attack on Puerto Rico had failed, and, worse still, it was made evident that, as Hawkins had foreseen, every Spanish settlement of importance would be fully prepared to receive the rovers.

Unable to do more at Puerto Rico, Drake sailed to the Carribean coast and took the town of La Hacha, which the inhabitants agreed to ransom for thirty-four thousand ducats. The people of Rancheria, a village on the coast, also offered to pay a ransom; but the governor, a gallant and patriotic Don, flatly refused his consent, and told Drake to his face he could do as he pleased but that not a penny should he have. Rancheria accordingly was burned to the ground, and several other villages shared the same fate.

Meanwhile the troops, and the crews of the ships, were suffering heavily from disease; neither did the officers escape, and not a day passed but some poor fellows were consigned to the deep. It would have been far better had the squadron set sail for England, but Drake would not confess to defeat; he knew how much both Elizabeth and her people reckoned upon the expedition, and he sternly resolved that they should not be disappointed. Accordingly he steered his course for Nombre de Dios, which, after a brief resistance from the few Spanish soldiers who garrisoned it, was captured.

Here again the wearied band met with keen disappointment. The inhabitants had fled and the town was desolate. With the exception of a little gold and silver, and a few pearls, no booty was to be discovered, and the destruction of the town and the vessels in the harbour could have afforded the invaders but meagre satisfaction.

There remained one other place at which the baffled admiral might retrieve his laurels and turn failure into success. At that time Panama was a storehouse for the precious metals. The products of the Peruvian mines were transported to Panama to be kept until opportunity offered for their carriage to Spain. The idea of capturing this treasure cheered the drooping hearts of the men, who gladly undertook the tedious and dangerous march across the isthmus.

Seven hundred and fifty of the strongest and bravest soldiers were chosen for the risky enterprise, and Sir Thomas Baskerville himself commanded them. But the ill-luck which had thus far dogged the expedition attended it still. For two days the harassed adventurers marched over the rough and broken ground and through narrow defiles, where they were assailed by volleys of shot from unseen marksmen who hid in the neighbouring woods.

It was discovered also that strong forts, stoutly manned, had been erected to bar their passage, and, being unable to force a way, they returned to their ships, having lost nearly a hundred men in the disastrous enterprise. As an old writer quaintly phrased it : " They had so much at their breakfast, they thought they should surfeit with a dinner and supper of the same."

This final failure was the crowning blow. By

this time the men were in a miserable state of destitution; their food had long since given out—they were nearly starved, and disease mowed them down in scores. Several officers, Drake's most intimate friends, had died of wounds or illness, and the admiral was compelled to abandon any further attempt on the Spanish settlements in America.

It is a melancholy picture this of the storm-battered vessels, with only half their crews alive, and those dying of disease and starvation; while the admiral himself, the brilliant sailor whose fame was world-wide, lay in his cabin, or moved about feebly, dying before the eyes of the rugged men who loved him.

"These regions are sadly changed from what they were in former times," he declared. "I once found delicious and pleasant harbours, but it now seemeth a waste and barren wilderness."

The shadow of death lay darkly upon him, but the gallant spirit was not easily quenched. "It matters not, my men," said he, "God hath many things in store for us. I know many means to do her Majesty good service, and to make us rich; for we must have gold before we see England."

More bitter than death must have been the thought to him that they should return to Plymouth harbour, where he had received so many enthusiastic welcomes, and have to confess that they had been balked in their object. It must not be said that Francis Drake had been baffled by the hated Spaniards. So from time

to time the old hero buoyed up his spirits with
the hope that they would intercept some rich
galleon and make themselves masters of her
valuable treasure.

But the days wore on, and no prize fell to them
except a vessel or two of small account. Another
captain died, and now Drake, too feeble for
exercise, took to his cabin. Soon he grew worse,
a fever seized him, and it became plain that
his weakened constitution could no longer battle
successfully against the dread disease.

From the accounts given by the old writers,
it is not difficult to conjure up a picture of the
last sad scene. A vision of the cabin rises before
our eyes, and we see the worn warrior tossing on
his couch, carefully tended by his officers and the
ship's surgeon. It is early morning of January 28,
1596, and a flicker of added strength comes to the
dying man. He yearns to be in the open air
again, to walk the deck, to look upon the faces
of his devoted soldiers.

With an effort he rises from his couch and
endeavours to dress himself. The exertion is too
much—he reels and staggers against the side of
the cabin; strange words issue from his lips;
he glances around wildly, and sinks helplessly
into the hands of the surgeon. His attendants
carry him tenderly and with reverence to his
couch, and then, standing in silence, wait for the
end, which they know cannot be long delayed.
Once he opens his eyes, and his lips move as
if in speech; but it is his final effort, and the
next moment Sir Francis Drake is dead.

The little squadron, shrouded in gloom, proceeded to Porto Bella, an island not far distant
from the mainland, and there cast anchor in the
bay. The death of the admiral filled the sailors
with dejection, for, whatever may be said of
Drake, it is certain that he was loved and
idolised by his men.

Sir Thomas Baskerville, who now became the
leader, decided that the expedition should return
to England without delay. But there was one
mournful ceremony to be performed : the body
of the dead sea-king must be committed to
the deep. A solemn service was held, and then,
amidst volleys of musketry and the firing of all
the big guns, the body, enclosed in a leaden
coffin, was reverently lowered over the side of
the flagship. Not far from the place where he
first won fame and fortune, the old hero was laid
to his rest.

The squadron, after a sharp fight with a
Spanish fleet on the way, reached England in
the beginning of May 1596, with the melancholy
news that it had failed in its object, and that
its two chiefs — the ablest sea-captains in the
world—were dead.

Sir Francis Drake was short in stature, but
broad and sturdy, with deep chest and strong
limbs. His hair was brown, he had large clear
eyes, and altogether a prepossessing appearance.
In working his way up the ladder of fame he
had made numerous enemies, and many hard
things were spoken and written of him both
before and after his death. He was charged with

piracy, with a love of show and a desire for popularity, and with an overweening ambition; but friends and foes were alike in their judgment that a more skilful or more daring sailor never navigated a ship or boarded a hostile craft.

Fuller describes him as "a very religious man, chaste in his life, just in his dealings, true of his word, merciful to those who were under him, and hating nothing so much as idleness : he was never wont to rely on other men's care, how trusty or skilful soever they might seem to be, but always despising danger and refusing no toil ; he was wont himself to be one (whoever was a second) at every turn where courage, skill or industry was to be employed."

One of his generous acts was the founding, with the assistance of Sir John Hawkins, of the "Chest" at Chatham, for the purpose of relieving the wants of old and wounded sailors. In 1884, this institution was removed to Greenwich and has always been a source of untold good to our naval seamen.

In spite of his faults, and we do not claim that he was a stainless knight, Englishmen will ever remember Drake as one of our most glorious sea-kings. He was the first of our race to sail round the world, and he was the first and foremost of the gallant band that by their courage, skill, and splendid audacity, helped to make England the Mistress of the Seas.

ROBERT BLAKE.

There lay the Sound and the Island with green leaves down
*   beside the water,*
* The town, the Hoe, the masts, with sunset fired—*
Dreams! ay, dreams of the dead! for the great heart faltered
*   on the threshold,*
* And darkness took the land his soul desired.*

ROBERT BLAKE,

ADMIRAL AND GENERAL AT SEA.

CHAPTER I.

A Sturdy Roundhead.

IN the year 1640, the long and bitter disputes between Charles I. and his Parliament came to a head : the king raised the royal standard at Nottingham, called the loyal gentry to his aid, and resolved by force of arms to re-establish his power. To his side flocked the majority of the nobles and landed proprietors in the kingdom—men of high birth, of rank and wealth, to whom loyalty was as sacred as religion, and who were ready to sacrifice, with a joyous abandon, money and goods and life itself for the royal cause.

Opposed to them were small farmers, labourers, artisans, students, traders, clerks, and the bulk of the citizens in the large towns. These men were unskilled in arms, and unused to the terrors of the battlefield, but they were equally brave, courageous, and devoted to their principles. Many were filled with a stern religious enthusiasm, and deep down in their hearts lay the conviction that

in fighting against Charles they were doing battle
for the Lord of Hosts Himself.

At this memorable period in our history there
was living at Bridgwater, unknown and unnoticed
beyond his narrow circle of friends and neighbours, a man whose name was within a few years
to be celebrated throughout the civilised world,
and the lustre of whose achievements has remained
undimmed for centuries.

Robert Blake was born at Bridgwater in 1599,
the son of Humphrey Blake and of Sara Williams,
a wealthy lady who brought to her husband the
valuable estate of Plansfield. The Blakes were an
old West of England family, and Robert's father
was an adventurous merchant, who sailed in his
own ship to foreign lands, anxious to trade peace-
ably, but ever ready to defend his vessel and
goods against the attack of an enemy.

In those days the sailor's life was far from being
monotonous. The merchant was really an adventurer, beset by perils from the moment of weighing
anchor until his storm-tossed craft crept safely
back to port. He had to guard against not only
the dangers of storm and tempest, and of unseen
rocks, but fierce pirates of every nation who
swarmed in the narrow seas waiting to pounce
upon any weak and helpless vessel. As in the
days of Elizabeth, so now—not a ship left port
but it carried one or more pieces of cannon, while
every man of the crew was fully armed.

Many a strange tale of daring and derring-do
young Robert must have listened to in the quaint
old west-country town, but it does not appear that

he evinced any inclination to follow his father's calling. He was a silent, thoughtful lad, with a taste rather for a life of study than for one of stirring adventure, and he was an earnest pupil in the grammar-school of his native town.

Thus the first sixteen years of his life passed quietly enough, and then he pursued his studies at Oxford, where he remained for several years, taking the usual degrees, but not otherwise distinguishing himself.

Meanwhile, affairs had been going not too happily at Bridgwater. Several of his father's voyages had met with ill-success; difficulties began to increase, and at length Robert, sacrificing his cherished dreams of a literary life, returned home to devote himself to his parents. In the next year his father died, and on Robert devolved the responsibility of managing the estate, and of seeing to the welfare of his numerous brothers and sisters. This task he undertook cheerfully, for it was a duty; and few men have ever clung more closely to what they considered duty than did Robert Blake.

From the very beginning of the trouble with the king, Blake ranged himself on the side of the Parliament—as, indeed, his religious opinions compelled him to do; and when Charles, after a lapse of several years, summoned a fresh Parliament, Blake was sent to attend its meetings as the member for Bridgwater. This Parliament, however, was soon dissolved, and Blake returned home, feeling convinced that before long the dispute would be settled by force of arms.

The raising of the royal standard at Nottingham brought the peaceful portion of his life to an end; rightly or wrongly, he had chosen his part in opposition to the King, and from that moment began the marvellous career which was to set his name high up on the list of English heroes and leaders.

It would be out of place here to attempt to trace the course of the Civil War in detail: we must content ourselves with describing the main incidents with which our hero was most intimately connected. The troop which he raised among his friends and neighbours, was one of the first in the field, and it rendered conspicuous service in the western country for the Parliamentary arms.

Blake himself, though wholly unversed in the art of war, speedily displayed the skill and talent of a veteran leader. At the head of his men he scoured the country, disheartening the Royalists and cheering his friends wherever he appeared. The reputation thus acquired was soon afterwards heightened by the brave defence of his post at Bristol against heavy odds.

This important city was held for the Parliament by Colonel Fiennes, with two thousand soldiers, among whom was Captain Blake, who had charge of a strong fort at Prior's Hill. The capture of Bristol would be of tremendous advantage to the king, and accordingly he sent thither his warlike and dashing nephews, Prince Rupert and Prince Maurice, with fourteen thousand foot, six thousand horse, and a number of cannon. Encamping at Clifton, Rupert summoned the garrison to surrender, and, finding his appeal disregarded, prepared for assault.

The first attack failed, but early the next morning the Royalists again advanced, and this time a determined attempt was made to capture the fort at Prior's Hill. Again and again the Royalists, with almost incredible bravery, rushed forward, but only to be hurled back by a steady and well-directed fire. Animated by their leader's heroism, the garrison stuck to their guns, dealing out death in every direction; but the assailants were not to be denied.

Led by Lord Grandison, they rushed up boldly in face of the murderous fire and swarmed into the shallow ditch surrounding the fort. Stern and undaunted, Blake maintained his position until the enemy once more retired in confusion; then, calling on his men to follow, he let down the drawbridge and hurled his small force against the flying foe. Rallied by their leaders, the retreating Royalists once more faced round, when a fierce hand-to-hand encounter took place, resulting in a complete victory for the stubborn Roundheads.

As it chanced, this brave defence of Prior's Hill did not save the city from capture. In another part the assailants forced the defences, and the governor, losing heart, agreed to surrender his post on condition that his troops were permitted to march out unmolested, leaving their arms and ammunition to the victors. Blake was extremely angry at this news, which did not reach him for some hours, and at first was extremely

unwilling to obey ; but finally he threw open the
gates and surrendered the fort which he had
defended so gallantly.

By this time his value began to be appreciated :
he was made a lieutenant-colonel, and ordered
to strengthen the garrison at Lyme, a small
fishing town built in a narrow valley and over-
looked on three sides by hills.   Into this obscure
place, defended by a dry ditch, a few earthworks,
and three small batteries, he flung his handful of
soldiers and prepared with vigour and energy to
hold his post against all comers.

That Lyme could be defended successfully no
Royalist and few Roundheads believed, and
Prince Maurice, who swept down from the
Somerset hills with an imposing army, summoned
the garrison to surrender without a thought of
defiance.   He was speedily undeceived : Blake
scornfully refused to abandon his charge, and
when the Royalist horse rode down on the lines,
he hurled them back in utter confusion.   Then
in deep columns the infantry advanced, but with
no better success.   They were brave and loyal
men, but the most splendid bravery could avail
little in face of the hot fire poured in by the
defenders, who, thanks to their leader's wise
precautions, possessed ample cover.

The attempt to capture the town by storm
having thus signally failed, Maurice was compelled to undertake its subjection by a regular
siege.   The Royalists went to work with a will :
day after day they hammered the forts with their
cannon ; on the land side they shut the garrison

up closely, and from time to time stormed the breastworks with unexampled heroism. Once an advance-guard actually forced the lines ; but the main body having been repulsed, those who had entered the town were cut off, and they died fighting to the last.

Then it appeared as if famine would at length effect what sword and fire had been unable to accomplish ; but, just as the stock of flour came to an end, a fleet of ships was observed in the offing lying as near the shore as the shallowness of the water would permit. The vessels were under the command of the Earl of Warwick, a Parliamentary officer who had brought the resolute garrison a small supply of provisions, to which the sailors added by giving up a large portion of their own rations for the use of their heroic but half-starved comrades.

Another assault resulted in disaster to the be-siegers, and then Blake, as cunning in strategy as he was brave in action, devised a scheme which had the effect of ending the siege. Three hundred sailors were landed secretly, and Warwick then sailed along the coast as if searching for a favourable spot at which to disembark a portion of his fighting-men.

Now, as Blake had foreseen, Prince Maurice jumped to the conclusion that part of the garrison had been embarked for the purpose of landing again elsewhere and attacking his forces in the rear. With this notion in his head, Maurice despatched his cavalry to watch the vessels and prevent a landing, while with the rest of his force he made a determined attack on what he conceived to be the weakened garrison.

This, the final assault, was the most terrible of all. The very flower of the Royalist troops were in the forefront, and they rushed to the charge as if resolved to conquer or die. So furious was their onset that even the sturdy Roundheads were borne back a space; but every house in the narrow, tortuous streets served them as a fortress, and from windows and doorways volley after volley was poured into the thick of the advancing lines.

But the blood of King Charles's men was hot, and they would not be denied. Cheering and shouting they forced a passage; the smoke and flames of burning houses ascended skywards; the men of the garrison were weary and well-nigh exhausted; in spite of the three hundred sailors, it seemed as if the persistent daring of Prince Maurice would be rewarded by a striking and decisive victory.

But the Roundhead colonel averted this calamity. He drew back his men—as the tiger withdraws for a deadlier spring—and then, having completed his arrangements, returned with grim determination. Well and valiantly fought the Cavaliers, but their heroism availed naught. Steadily but surely they were borne back, until, when night fell, more than five hundred of King Charles's bravest followers lay dead in the streets and in the outskirts of Lyme.

CHAPTER II.

The Defence of Taunton.

THE brilliant defence of what Charles called a "vile little fishing town" had dealt the King's cause a severe blow. While Maurice's fine army had been employed in attempting the reduction of Lyme, the Earl of Essex, who commanded the Parliamentary forces, had marched westward from London, gathering fresh troops at all the towns through which he passed.

Disturbed by the approach of this new body of foes, and unwilling to risk a pitched battle, Maurice, calling in his adherents from the surrounding districts, together with a large part of the garrison of Taunton, marched towards Exeter and was closely followed by Essex, who had fond but vain hopes of smiting his fiery opponent hip and thigh.

Now, the far west with few exceptions stood stoutly for the King, and Charles, who then lay at Oxford with his army, resolved on making a rapid march westward in order to place Essex between two fires. It may be mentioned in passing that the King accomplished this feat, and, joining Maurice at Liskeard, shut up Essex in a desolate corner whence the baffled general escaped by sea, leaving his troops worn out, half starved, surrounded, and outnumbered, with no other course than to surrender to the victorious Cavaliers.

Having thus disposed of the Roundhead army, Charles, but for one man, would have reigned undisputed master of the west. All the most important towns were in his possession; the castles and strongholds were garrisoned by his troops; his horsemen scoured the country in every direction, preventing those who were on the side of the Parliament from raising a hand in its behalf.

The man who kept the Puritan cause alive in the west, was the same daring soldier who, by his military skill and personal courage, had baffled Prince Maurice at Lyme. Blake had observed with intense grief and amazement how Essex was gradually getting himself into the toils, and had looked about for a means of affording him assistance. This, he thought, could best be done by the capture of Taunton, then in the hands of the King's forces.

This town was a place of considerable importance; it commanded the highway leading westward, and through it lay the shortest, almost the only practicable, route to the west. If the Roundheads held Taunton, the King's troops might be prevented from joining Maurice, and Essex would have time to extricate himself from his difficult position. It was a bold game to play, but Blake was used to vigorous measures. His men believed in him, loved and trusted him, and were ready to attempt whatever he wished without question or murmur.

Taunton, as we have said, was held by the Royalists; but the citizens, on the whole, did not favour the King's cause, nor were they likely to make any sacrifice on his behalf. Colonel Reeves, who commanded the garrison, knew this, and, when Blake suddenly appeared, he felt unable to offer any strenuous opposition. Blake allowed him to march off to Bridgwater with his troops, and then, amidst the clanging of bells and the joyous welcome of the citizens, the triumphant Roundheads rode in.

This dashing and brilliant capture did not save the Earl of Essex from defeat, but it raised the spirits of the Roundheads, while Taunton served as a rallying-point for all those of the west who were against the King. The news of this remarkable exploit soon reached London, where it was hailed with joyous acclamation by people and Parliament, and the successful raider was instantly appointed to the office of governor. But the hazardous feat of taking the town was far less difficult than holding it.

Before the surrender of the Roundhead army in Cornwall, the new governor, indeed, had little to fear. At the head of a scanty troop he raided the country far and near, cutting up convoys, capturing prisoners, and securing arms, ammunition, and much needed provisions.

No danger daunted him or his men, and fatigue was a word the meaning of which they did not understand. No district was safe from them ; no weak body of the enemy could march a mile without the disagreeable prospect of a swift and sudden swoop from Blake and his riders, and the garrisons of the numerous castles and fortified houses for miles around were forced to be on the alert continually.

But Robert Blake, with all his daring intrepidity, was far from being a rash and headstrong soldier. He was a shrewd, level-headed man with a faculty for looking ahead ; he knew Essex must be crushed, and guessed that, as soon as that object was accomplished, the enemy would turn their attention to Taunton.   In this he was correct, for, although Charles himself, elated by his success, could think of little but a victorious march toward London, he deputed Colonel Wyndham to reduce the rebellious town to obedience.

The future admiral foresaw and prepared for what must inevitably prove a bitter and desperate struggle.   Taunton was not a place that could be defended easily.   It was unwalled ; its fortifications were ancient and in poor repair ; it was shut in on every side by hills, and ringed round by hostile strongholds.   In course of time provisions must fail, and the only means of securing fresh supplies was by hazardous sallies.

Blake knew all these things well ; but he had counted the cost, had chosen his part, and nothing but the absolute commands of his superiors would have induced him to abandon his post.   Fortunately for the Parliamentary cause he was left to his own devices, and he waited with calm and steady resolution for the approach of the foe.

At first the Royalists made their appearance in small and semi-independent bands, riding round the town—scouring and laying waste the country districts, carrying off cattle, but not venturing on an assault. This was but the beginning of the stubborn contest, and, though annoying, productive of little real harm to the garrison. Suddenly Colonel Wyndham arrived with a small force, which he had brought from Bridgwater. He was a fellow-townsman of Blake, and possessed few misgivings as to the result of the encounter. He little knew the man with whom he was about to cross swords.

This was the answer the Roundhead colonel sent to his imperious summons to surrender: "These are to let you know, that, as we neither fear your menaces, nor accept your proffers, we wish you for the time to come to desist from all overtures of the like nature unto us, who are resolved to the last drop of our blood to maintain the quarrel we have undertaken; and I doubt not but the same God who hath hitherto protected us, will bless us with an issue answerable to the justice of our cause; however, to Him alone shall we stand or fall."

Once more Wyndham sent a messenger, pointing out the weakness of the defence, and urging that, as Taunton must fall, it would be better to yield without bloodshed. Blake smiled grimly in answer, and the wonderful duel began. As at Lyme, so here—the odds were so overwhelming against the defenders that few people in either Royalist or Roundhead camp believed that the garrison could hold out for any length of time. But the governor had prepared his plans skilfully, and his own splendid character had gained for him the love and devotion of his men. To please him they would have flung away their lives without a murmur.

Fortunately for the citizens, the surrounding hills were too far off to be of any advantage to the enemy's artillery, while their own castle stood on rising ground near the centre of the town. It was partly in ruins, but it still had its walls and gates and was protected also by a double moat. Blake strengthened the castle walls, erected strong barricades across the roads, placed a portion of his artillery near the east gate, and garrisoned the commanding houses with his bravest and most accurate marksmen. Best of all, he infused a part of his own fearlessness and devotion to duty into the hearts of his devoted followers.

After a slight skirmish, which ended disastrously for his side, Colonel Wyndham resolved upon a strict blockade, hoping to effect by starvation what might prove a serious task in any other way. Accordingly his troops were skilfully posted in a ring, the roads were cut up and barricaded in order to prevent the passage of vehicles, and the besiegers awaited the result with the utmost confidence. They knew full well that in a fight with starvation even the bravest men must succumb.

But Blake was a man not easily daunted. He took stock of his provisions, placed his troops on scantier rations, and did everything in his power to prevent waste or extravagance. Every pound of bread was as much a weapon in his armoury

Frontispiece.

as a sharp sword or a loaded musket. Nor did he remain tamely behind his rude lines of defence. At frequent intervals part of the garrison sallied forth, fell vigorously on the nearest foes, broke the cordon, swept the surrounding district, and returned in triumph laden with corn and vegetables, and driving droves of captured cattle before them.

But these resources could not last indefinitely, and many an anxious hour the Roundhead leader must have spent on his watch-tower looking for help which did not arrive. Still there was no despair either in his breast or in the breasts of his stubborn followers. Knowing what a blow their gallant defence must deal to the King's cause, they were resolved to endure to the end. And at last the succour for which they had waited so patiently, came. A body of Roundhead horse, riding secretly but swiftly, fell upon the besiegers' line, snapped the cordon like pack-thread, and galloped in triumph along the streets of Taunton.

Panic-stricken by this sudden and unexpected blow, the enemy still staggered in amazement, when Blake, with that promptitude in action which was so pre-eminently a part of his nature, selected the stoutest of his garrison, joined hands with the newcomers, and swept down on the besieging regiments in a whirlwind of fury. The fight was sharp while it lasted; but very soon the enemy were in full retreat, and their flight was hastened by the stern troopers, who chased them like deer until they found shelter in

Bridgwater. The hunted had become the hunter, and it was well for the new quarry that a place of safety was at hand.

The effect of this remarkable exploit was speedily apparent. The Royalists, abandoning the open country, retired to their strongholds, while Blake rode triumphantly hither and thither, raising the hopes of his friends and striking terror into the hearts of his foes. For some time he remained almost undisputed master of the fair west country. So complete was his success that the King, fearing he would relieve Weymouth, which the royal forces were then besieging, ordered Lord Goring down there in hot haste.

That fiery Royalist, however, failed to capture the little stronghold, and presently, with an army of 10,000 men, he marched through Somerset towards Wells, exciting the utmost consternation among all those who were favourable to the popular cause. Numbers of aged men, women and children carrying what valuables they possessed, fled at his approach and made their way to Taunton, in the full belief that where Blake was there they would find safety. He received them with open arms, and gave them quarters in the half-ruined houses.

Meanwhile, he continued his brilliant raiding, appearing now here, now there, always in the most unexpected places, and keeping the whole country-side in a continual state of alarm and turmoil. It soon became plain to the King's advisers, and to Charles himself, that while Blake kept possession of Taunton there would

be no peace in the west, and that its reduction
was a matter of the most pressing importance.
Wyndham had failed utterly, and another leader
was now chosen in the person of the fierce and
able but unscrupulous Lord Goring. The first
act in the drama had been brought to a conclusion ; the second was about to begin.

CHAPTER III.

A Grim Struggle.

FREQUENT meetings, at which hot and bitter
words were spoken, were held between the
Royalist leaders. Some argued that their
troops could be more profitably employed than
by sitting down before Taunton ; others—west-
country Cavaliers, for the most part—urged that
it was a shame and a disgrace to allow the
Roundheads to remain masters of the situation.
They were for collecting a large army and for
throwing it day after day at the rebellious town.

Their views finally prevailed, and Lord Goring
drew up a plan of action. His proposal was to
post a portion of his army in a position to thwart
any relief-force, and to draw a tight cordon
with his foot and artillery, covered by several
squadrons of his bravest horsemen. Sir Richard
Grenville was ordered to march with his troops—
to the number of over 3000—and huge magazines
of stores and ammunition were established.

The brief period of liberty for the sorely-tried

citizens was at an end; every road was occupied by the enemy, and the trenches within a few hundred yards of the suburbs were filled with Grenville's men. Goring, too, soon made his appearance with a large force, and once more the alarm-bells clanged, calling the garrison to arms. Goring pressed on doggedly, fighting his way foot by foot to the gate at East Reach, while Grenville delivered assault after assault from the trenches.

Blake held out firmly, but he was in a very critical position, when news of the approach of the Roundhead general, Waller, caused Goring to march eastward. Expecting to fight a pitched battle, he ordered Grenville to join him, but Sir Richard bluntly refused to obey. He had vowed, he said, not to leave the trenches until Taunton was reduced, and he would not stir a foot. Threats and coaxings were alike useless: move he would not while the town still held out. The Cavalier knight was a grim fighter, and no doubt he honestly believed that the place must soon fall; but his stubborn opposition made things awkward for his own side, and another meeting was hastily summoned.

Who should give way—Goring or Grenville? The wordy war was kindled afresh, and, meanwhile, the intrepid Blake taking advantage of the opportunity continued strengthening his defences and making fierce and vigorous sallies. But his peril was hourly increasing; his enemies came to a fixed resolution. Cost what it might, Taunton should be subdued. For this purpose they would grudge neither men nor money : they would make an end of this troublesome opposition and be free to carry their victorious arms elsewhere in the King's behalf.

Once the decision was arrived at, no time was lost in putting it into execution. Colonel Wyndham was promptly recalled with his regiment; Goring's army was brought down with the whole of his artillery, and at length it really appeared as if the heroic garrison was doomed. But the governor kept a stout heart, and, in spite of the force opposed to him, superior in numbers, arms, and position, he had no thought of surrender.

The new siege began ominously for the Royalists. Five miles from Taunton stood Wellington House, into which Blake had thrown a small garrison. Thither the fiery Grenville, having first drawn a strong cordon round the town, proceeded. While closely examining the building with a view to planning an assault, he was wounded so dangerously that he had to be removed to Exeter, and his command was given to Sir John Berkeley.

But there was no respite for Blake and his gallant followers. Day succeeded day, and still the siege continued. Wellington House, after a splendid defence, was captured and destroyed ; the trenches were advanced nearer and nearer ; the pleasant suburbs were reduced to howling wilder-nesses ; smiling gardens were laid waste ; whole rows of houses were burned down ; neither by day nor by night was there a moment's peace for the harassed garrison or the wearied citizens.

Near the East Gate the fighting was incessant. With almost incredible bravery the Cavaliers surged again and again up to the very doors of the houses, garrisoned by Blake's best and stoutest men.   Cannon-ball and bullet swept the assailants down ; but the survivors would not be denied, and sheer strength alone hurled them back at last, broken and disorganised.   Even those people whose sympathies lay with the garrison praised the dauntless heroism of the King's friends.

The six days which Grenville had so confidently anticipated would witness an end to the fighting, lengthened into as many weeks, and, though the . assailants had gained temporary possession of a few ruined cottages, Taunton remained unsubdued.   And while we must not forget to give due praise to the sturdy garrison, there can be little doubt that the heart and soul of the defence was Robert Blake.

But again he was beset, and now by an enemy more dangerous even than the dashing Cavaliers. Famine began to stare him in the face !   Bread, we are told, was sold for twenty times its ordinary market value ; the troopers fought and watched, night and day, on the scantiest of scanty rations ; and the poorer citizens suffered terribly.   Holding off his forces for a brief period, Sir John Berkeley again proposed that the garrison should surrender ; but Blake, half in jest, half in earnest, replied that he could not think of abandoning his post while he still had a pair of boots to eat.

Then the fighting was resumed, and the Cavaliers, rendered desperate by the stubborn resistance, gave their enemy no peace. In the early morning— when the sun rode high in the heavens—in the dark watches of the night—the heavy cannon flung their ponderous missiles into the devoted place, and bands of men, burning with zeal and courage, rushed forward, pike in hand, in the effort to dislodge the defenders from their position. Fresh troops were brought up; ammunition was freely expended; the cordon was drawn more tightly so that no provisions could pass the lines; everything that skill and daring could devise was done by the King's troops.

The news of the marvellous defence spread throughout the country, and the citizens of London especially clamoured for the relief of the heroic garrison.

Now, while Blake was thus holding in check some of the King's most brilliant leaders, another eminent soldier was slowly and patiently moulding an army that was destined to bring the Great Rebellion to a successful issue. In the eastern counties Oliver Cromwell was steadily fashioning the New Model, and, as soon as his task was completed, several regiments were despatched under Colonel Welden post-haste towards Taunton. Volunteers eagerly flocked to join them on the way, but, even with these additions, Welden's force was far inferior in numbers to that which he was defiantly bearding.

Trusty scouts rode in advance to inform Blake that a relief-party was approaching, and to devise with him some means of signalling between the two friendly forces. The joyful news cheered the citizens, and every heart beat high with hope.

But Sir John Berkeley was not to be balked of his prey without a struggle. Failing to induce Blake to hazard a sortie, he gathered his men together for one tremendous attack, hoping to overwhelm the garrison before the arrival of the relief-party. The Cavaliers responded to his orders with even more than their usual dash and daring. Like their chief, they realised that if Taunton was ever to be captured it must be captured now, and with ringing cheers and cries of "God and the King!" they rushed to the assault. Like a hurricane wind they swept across the waste ground, carried the outposts by over-whelming strength, toppled over the first of the barricades, and, pike in hand, flung the defending Roundheads back.

Blake, playing a waiting game, kept his men well in hand. His stock of powder was running very low, and he had no wish that any of it should be used wastefully. But his picked marks-men, stationed in the half-ruined houses, caused the assailants heavy loss, and the brilliant Cavaliers, discouraged by the fall of so many of their comrades, began to press the charge less fiercely, and even to seek shelter from the volleys of musketry.

Blake, who watched the struggle with keen eyes, perceived these signs of weakness, and, like a skilful general, seized his opportunity. Calling up every available soldier, he placed himself at their head and advanced on the foe. In vain the Cavaliers essayed to stand their ground; in vain their bravest leaders rushed forward with shouts of defiance—the grim pikemen pursued their way, steadily and remorselessly, crushing all who opposed their progress. The Cavaliers had done their best—and had failed. The battle was lost, and at last, seeing further resistance to be useless, the survivors fled.

The weary garrison, however, although victorious, could not afford to rest. Sir John Berkeley had suffered a heavy defeat, but he still possessed a strong army, and he was not unlikely to attempt a surprise attack during the night. So Blake and his men, worn out and half famished though they were, kept vigil until the dawn, and then glorious news reached the weary watchers. The enemy were in full retreat! Blake, unable to believe the truth, concluded that Berkeley was endeavouring to draw him into a trap; but presently several scouts rode in at full speed to confirm the report.

Then the victorious commander was swift to take action. Bugles sounded; orders were issued; the troopers mounted and formed up, and, riding swiftly, swooped down on the enemy's rearguard like hawks swooping on their prey. A large quantity of arms and ammunition fell into their hands, and, with this much-needed booty, they returned in triumph to meet a portion of Welden's horse, which had galloped almost without pause to the succour of the beleaguered town.

Once more bonfires gaily blazed in London, and thanks were accorded by Parliament to all who had assisted in the stubborn defence or welcome relief. But Taunton was fated to endure even more misery. Lord Goring, who had been previously withdrawn from the west, was now ordered to return, and, falling suddenly on Colonel Welden, he drove that officer with his troops into the sorely-tried place.

Taunton was again isolated, and surrounded by a ring of armed foes; but Goring, having learned wisdom from Sir John Berkeley's defeats, did not attempt to capture it by storm. Instead, he contented himself with a vigorous blockade, and trusted to famine for success. But Blake now had a larger garrison under his command, and, although there were more mouths to be filled, there were more men to obtain provisions. By day and night bodies of cavalry issued forth, and, frequently evading the enemy's vigilance, scoured the surrounding country for food. Numerous brave men fell in this hazardous service, but generally the forays were successful, and supplies of provisions were thus obtained for the starving citizens.

Meanwhile, in other parts of the country the struggle was going steadily against the King. Cromwell's military skill and the bravery of his Ironsides were winning decisive victories, and at last Lord Fairfax, with a large Roundhead army, was enabled to turn his attention to the west. His march was rapid and brilliant in the extreme. Stronghold after stronghold fell into his hands; the Royalist bands melted away at his approach; even the redoubtable Goring was compelled to abandon the siege, and Taunton was once more free.

Blake's chief work now was to restore order in the ruined town, and to relieve the distress of the poorer citizens; but there was still one piece of fighting to be done before that part of the land had complete rest. Most of the fortresses had opened their gates to Fairfax's triumphant army, but Dunster Castle continued to fly the royal flag. Often attacked, it had never yet fallen, but Blake determined to carry it by storm.

The castle was immensely strong and in a splendid position, being built on the summit of a steep hill. The garrison answered the summons to surrender by a message of stern defiance, and for several days repulsed every attack. In vain the Roundheads rushed to the assault; they were hurled back in confusion, and, but for their leader's ingenuity, the massive castle would probably have remained untaken.

Realising the serious nature of the conflict, Blake secretly prepared a mine, which, when exploded, flung down a part of the walls and made wide breaches through which it was possible for his men to enter. The loyal garrison stood stoutly to their arms, but, inspired by their chief's heroic example, the stormers rushed on, and, after a terrific struggle, in which both sides suffered severely, Dunster Castle was finally won for the Parliament.

CHAPTER IV.

The Beginning of a Fierce Duel.

THE terrible Civil War, which began favourably for King Charles, ended, as we are all
aware, in his overthrow. The King fell into
the hands of his enemies, who were divided in
opinion as to what should be done with him.
Some cried aloud for his blood, urging that there
could be no peace while Charles Stuart remained
alive ; others desired that he should be deposed
and banished from the realm, which they held that
he had misruled.

Robert Blake had no wish to take the King's
life. He himself was a sincere republican, with
no liking for kings of any sort ; and he had done
more than one man's share in wrecking and over-
throwing the monarchy, but he had no ambition
to raise himself at the expense of a fallen foe.
While others strove to advance their position he
remained faithfully at his post, ready to do anything in his power for the welfare of his country,
but void of personal ambition. When his opinion
was asked, he gave it without fear or favour—no
more seeking to ingratiate himself with the new
chiefs than he had been anxious to obtain the
goodwill of his former sovereign.

To get at a man's actual motives is always a
difficult matter, but, as far as can be judged,
Robert Blake was a man who lived up to his
ideas. His notions may have been right or wrong

—that is a matter of opinion on which it is certain we shall not all think alike—but what he believed, that he tried to carry out to the best of his ability. He had no thought for rewards, and never lifted a finger to grasp the glittering honours which might easily have been his. Among Cavaliers and Roundheads were men who cared little for the cause they espoused—mere self-seekers, striving to obtain fame or fortune or both. Blake's conduct after the downfall of King Charles showed that he was not of these.

He spoke out boldly against the trial of the King, and it is probable that his downright honesty of purpose gained him many enemies among the members of his own party. But the man who had held Lyme against Prince Maurice, and Taunton against a host of foes, was not to be regarded lightly. He had numerous friends; his influence over the people was enormous; his soldiers were devoted to him, and would have obeyed his orders without the least scruple. He had shown, too, a military genius second only to that of Cromwell, and it was known that he was absolutely without fear.

An attempt to bribe such a man with glittering gewgaws would be sheer folly; to endeavour to thwart him might prove extremely dangerous. But there was one side on which the hero of Taunton was always assailable. Blake was a genuine patriot. He wished to see his country great, and free, and strong; he desired that she should hold up her head among the nations and gain the respect of all the world. For this he was ready at any time to endure peril and hardship, and to hazard his life gladly.

Now, during the early part of the Civil War, the English navy, though taking sides with the Parliament, had not been very much involved in the quarrel ; but, after the seizure of the King, many of the sailors began to murmur. They were quite willing and even anxious to curb his power, but they had no desire to exchange the monarchy for a commonwealth.

These views were shared by their commander, Admiral Batten, who, on more than one occasion, had proved himself a stout and dogged fighter. Now he declared in favour of the King, and with eleven ships of the fleet sailed away for the Dutch coast, where the Prince of Wales accorded him a hearty welcome.

The men on the other ships, however, refused to desert their flag, and for some months a series of engagements, which had no decisive results, were entered into by the two opposing sections of the fleet. Then Prince Rupert arrived to assume command of the ships which still held by the fortunes of the hapless Charles.

A halo of perhaps rather false glory surrounds the memory of this dashing Cavalier. We are apt to regard him as the *beau-ideal* of a soldier of fortune. His had been a stormy life : even as a boy the misfortunes of his father had made him a restless wanderer throughout Europe, and his sword had rarely remained long in its scabbard. He was brave to a fault, but rash and headstrong ; and his ill-balanced judgment had often robbed him of the fruits which his valour had won. Yet his daring made him a formidable enemy, as the new English Government was to discover afresh.

Rupert had few scruples, and never hesitated in his course. He always knew what he wanted, and lost no time in trying to obtain it. He took over his squadron at a period when the royal fortunes had sunk to their lowest ebb. He had no money with which to pay his sailors, and no country which he could call his own ; but he had supreme confidence in his own ability and a daring disregard of all laws. He sold one of his largest ships to the Dutch, expended the money thus obtained in ammunition, and began to prey openly on the commerce of all nations—English for choice.

He called himself admiral of King Charles's fleet ; his enemies denounced him as a pirate, and the English rulers tried their hardest to sweep him from the seas. But the Commonwealth leaders were no match for this daring and ingenious prince, who seemed equally at home on sea or on land. What was to be done? One man had proved himself the prince's superior ashore ; was it possible that he could do the same afloat? Those in authority thought he could, and thus it happened that Robert Blake was asked to plunge again into the turmoil of strife, and take upon himself the office of General and Admiral at Sea.

There may have been other motives also, but the hero of Taunton was not the man to ask questions when he saw his course clear. He readily agreed to hazard his hardly-won reputation on a new element, and to begin the dangerous duel with his formidable opponent. The two leaders were fairly matched; both were brave, able, and daring, but Blake had one advantage in that he acted solely from a sense of duty and a whole-hearted love of country.

His first care was to put his ships into a seaworthy condition, and to appease the anger of the sailors who suffered from want of pay and from bad food. In a short time they were as devoted to him as his soldiers had been. He showed himself to be no figure-head admiral, and not even a merely fighting admiral. He was a just and humane man, and he saw that his crews were fairly paid, and that they obtained all the comforts it was possible to procure.

He made them feel that he was one of themselves, and that no reasonable complaint on their part would be disregarded. In the stress of battle he was their fearless leader, having no object except to beat the enemy; but at all times he was the men's true friend, in whom they learned to put their trust.

To aid him two other admirals were appointed, Colonels Deane and Popham, and the three chiefs worked as one. The ships were overhauled; able captains were placed in command; ammunition was procured; and it could shortly be said with truth that the Commonwealth possessed a real navy fit to contend with that commanded by Prince Rupert.

The English fleet was divided into four squadrons, one of which was under Blake's special command. He was nearly fifty years of age when, in April 1649, he hoisted his flag for the first time as an English admiral. The Commonwealth had abolished the Union Jack, and their sailors fought under a plain red cross on a white ground.

Meanwhile, Rupert had been sweeping the narrow seas with his ships, plundering peaceful traders, and creating such alarm that numerous merchants kept their vessels in port rather than trust them within reach of the lawless Cavalier. He had established his headquarters at Kinsale, in Ireland, where he could always retreat after a successful sally.

The hopes of the Royalists leaped high; they conjured up a vision of renewing the war on more equal terms, and of bringing back the exiled family in triumph. But they were reckoning without Blake, who was doing for the navy what Cromwell had done with such signal success for the Parliamentary army.

The new admiral possessed little skill in seamanship, but he had a grand faculty for getting at the heart of things. He never waited for the enemy to come to him, but made it his business to seek the enemy. This he did now, and Rupert was disagreeably surprised, while returning from a successful cruise, to discover his old rival, bearing down on him, capturing one of his smartest frigates, and chasing the remainder pell-mell into Kinsale harbour.

There Rupert remained, fuming and fretting

at his enforced inactivity, but absolutely helpless. It must be admitted that the prince was not daunted, and more than once he proposed to cut his way at all risks through the blockading vessels. This hazardous feat his captains refused to attempt, and he lay in harbour until the approach of winter, when the victories of Cromwell, who had taken command of the land forces in Ireland, warned him that his position was fast becoming desperate.

Leaving the least valuable of his squadron in harbour, he stole out at the end of October with seven vessels. A furious gale had driven most of the hostile ships to the nearest ports for shelter, so that the intrepid Rupert slipped safely away, and, plundering all the traders he fell in with on his voyage, steered a course to the river Tagus, where he was afforded protection by the King of Portugal.

Blake now enjoyed a brief spell of peace ; but very soon the Government, disturbed by the accounts of Rupert's doings, fitted out a small force of five ships, to which four more were afterwards added, and entrusted the command to Blake. He was given instructions to seek and destroy the escaped squadron, and to uphold the dignity of England on the high seas.

With as little delay as possible the admiral set sail, and when Rupert, early in the spring, dropped down the river for another roving cruise, he found, much to his surprise, his passage barred by the fleet of his veteran antagonist.

The King of Portugal was now in an awkward

position. Rupert had been feted, and caressed, and assured of Portuguese protection; but here was the English admiral demanding permission to fall on his enemy, and his fame as a fighter had already spread to Portugal. The puzzled king hesitated; changed front several times, endeavoured to hoodwink the English sailor, and finally declared that he would protect the prince with his whole available force.

Blake at once seized nine Portuguese ships coming from the harbour and added them to his own squadron, which so angered the king that he ordered his admiral to combine with Rupert and crush this insolent foe.

All through the autumn, however, the English maintained their position, and, intercepting a Brazil fleet of twenty-three sail, sank or captured all but the very smallest ships. This roused the King of Portugal to a fit of violent anger, and he again ordered his fleet to join with that of Prince Rupert and chase their enemy from the mouth of the Tagus.

It was much easier to issue this command than to execute it. Blake maintained his position, riding the seas in perfect safety, until at last the king, becoming alarmed, made his peace with England and ordered his now unwelcome guest to quit Portugal. Taking prompt advantage of the temporary absence of the hostile ships, Rupert hoisted his flag, weighed anchor, and slipped quietly down the river. Once more his persistent enemy had forced him adrift to live as best he could.

CHAPTER V.

The End of the Duel.

WHEN Blake returned to the Tagus, Rupert had vanished, but news of him was speedily to hand. After various adventures the prince sailed to Malaga, where he found six English merchant vessels lying under the protection of a Spanish battery. But the Spaniards were not ill-pleased to see their ancient enemies fighting among themselves, and not a gun of the battery was discharged when Rupert sailed boldly into the harbour.

Blake was cruising off the coast of Spain when a messenger reached him with the information that Rupert had plundered and burned six ships lying in Malaga harbour. Without doubt or hesitation the resolute admiral decided on his course. Between him and Rupert it was now a fight to a finish. Henceforth foreign powers would protect the pirates—for it must be remembered the Roundheads regarded the prince as a mere pirate—at their peril.

Leaving his lieutenants instructions, he headed his own particular squadron for the Mediterranean. Rupert had left Malaga, but the admiral was not to be balked in his quest. A fierce storm arose, but, if Rupert could ride through it safely, Blake could. On he swept, picking up a little confused information here and there until he learned that his enemy had run for shelter into Cartagena.

Thither the admiral sailed, and, to his delight, discovered the report to be correct.

Rupert, however, was not there. His ship, and that commanded by his brother Maurice, had parted from the main body in the gale; but of this, Blake at the time was ignorant. Instantly he sent ashore and explained to the governor the nature of his errand. The Spaniard replied that the vessels then in harbour were English ships, and, as England was at peace with Spain, he could not allow them to be in any way molested.

If by this reply he expected to frighten the Englishman from his prey, he was altogether mistaken. The Spaniards could act as friends or foes—the choice was theirs—but he intended destroying the vessels even had the whole might of Spain been arrayed against him.

Blake was a man of action rather than of words, and he did not love to shilly-shally. To his thinking the case was clear and admitted of no argument. Leaving the Spanish governor to do as he thought fit, the admiral issued his orders and bore into the harbour.

The encounter was sharp but short. One vessel was quickly overpowered, a second burned, and all the others were driven ashore in a state of hopeless ruin. Then, having demanded and obtained their stores and ammunition, he sailed away in pursuit of the two princes. Perhaps it was a masterful act, but Blake was a masterful man, and the Commonwealth owed everything to men of his character.

The chase now developed into a game of hide-and-seek, and a long while elapsed before the admiral learned that the brothers were lying quietly at anchor at Toulon, the strong naval station in the south of France. Thither he quickly followed, and immediately sent a message to the governor complaining of the shelter given to the enemies of the English Commonwealth. The governor treated the complaint with indifference, but he was speedily brought to his senses.

"Very well," said Blake; "if you choose to shelter pirates who prey on English ships, I shall capture all the French merchant vessels that come in my way."

This was a very unpleasant threat, and, as people were beginning to realise that this resolute admiral always kept his word, the governor thought it wise to rid Toulon of his dangerous visitors. Accordingly he furnished them with arms, ammunition, and stores, and at the first favourable opportunity they ran out. Passing through the Straits of Gibraltar, they steered their course to the West Indies. Some time afterwards their vessels parted company in a violent storm, and Maurice was never seen again. It is supposed his ship foundered, and that all on board were drowned.

Meanwhile, Blake's hands were full in keeping the seas for England, in protecting English commerce from the attacks of privateers, and in capturing French vessels as a punishment to the French for assisting privateers to prey on English shipping. On one occasion he met a French frigate, and signalled for the captain to come on board. The Frenchman complied, and was surprised to learn that he was a prisoner. Being a brave man, he refused to surrender his sword, and Blake, admiring his obstinacy, sent him back to his ship, giving him an opportunity to make a fight of it, which he did for two hours before being compelled to strike his flag.

Blake now returned home, where he was received with great enthusiasm by all who upheld the Commonwealth, and with respect and esteem even by those who still stood by the fallen monarch. For it could not be denied that this man, who had displayed skill and bravery and a dogged resolution during the Civil War, had shown the same characteristics at sea, and had well and worthily maintained the honour and reputation of his native country.

He had long since broken Rupert's power as a formidable enemy, but he had yet to deal the final blow. During the early days of his career at sea, Rupert, with wise forethought, had converted the Scilly Isles into a stronghold so powerful as to be considered impregnable. The prince was now far away, but the stronghold was in the capable hands of Sir John Grenville, a bold and intrepid Royalist who had on many previous occasions displayed the greatest daring. Grenville met the admiral's summons to surrender with defiance, declaring that he was prepared to hold his post against all comers.

Blake, as usual, wasted no more words. The largest of the Scilly Isles is St. Mary's, and close to it is Tresco, which was strongly garrisoned. Into Tresco the admiral poured his pikemen, led by Captain Morris. The garrison endeavoured to prevent a landing, but the stormers jumped into the water, waded ashore, and, pausing only to form, dashed at the ramparts.

They had no easy task; their fiery opponents fought them with pike, sword, and pistol, making them pay dearly for every foot of ground gained; but the assailants, pressing on stubbornly, made good their position, and at night the baffled Cavaliers, unable to continue their resistance longer, boarded their boats and passed over to St. Mary's. Thus far, the assault had been successful, but the remainder of the enterprise was even more hazardous.

St. Mary's rose steeply skyward, fringed with frowning rocks and strengthened by numerous forts. Had their opponent been any one but Blake, the Royalists might well have considered their position secure. But that rugged seaman soon gave them cause for thought. Without any delay he established a battery on Tresco, which not only did considerable damage, but effectually prevented the defenders from obtaining outside help, had such been available. Unless they stormed Tresco and defeated the garrison there, their doom was sealed.

Anxious not to waste time, the admiral next decided on a step which in those days was counted bold and hazardous in the extreme. By wonderful skill of seamanship he managed to bring his frigates through the narrow, dangerous channels,

"The stormers jumped into the water."

when he immediately opened fire on the castle. The shore guns answered with their terrific thunder, and all day long the tremendous artillery duel continued. The next morning it began again, and presently the fire from the frigates knocked down a portion of the massive wall.

This was enough for Blake. The guns had opened a way; his men would finish the business by sheer force of steel. He issued his orders; the pikemen sprang to the front with a cheer; all were eager and willing for the conflict, when Sir John Grenville, recognising that his power for a successful defence had vanished, agreed to surrender. A treaty was soon drawn up and signed, and the plucky garrison yielded themselves prisoners of war with all their arms, stores, and ammunition.

One other enterprise remained before the power of the King's friends was finally crushed. The Channel Islands were in their possession, and the governor, Sir George Carteret, was one of the finest soldiers who had ever done battle for the royal cause. He had established himself in Jersey—an island dangerous of approach owing to sunken rocks, and with a steep coast, against which a stormy sea ever thundered.

The island was dotted with strong forts and towers, while on a massive rock in St. Aubin's Bay, about a mile from St. Helier's, the capital of Jersey, stood Elizabeth Castle, where Sir George commanded.

In the beginning of the struggle it appeared as if Blake had at last met his match. He instantly

endeavoured to effect a landing, but the raging
surf and the heavy seas foiled him. Again he
tried, and was for the second time baffled. The
sea, which had so often befriended him, here
proved his enemy. Two boats, filled with daring
soldiers, were caught in the furious surf and
broken into matchwood. Then the admiral recalled his troops and began a cannonade, which
had no result.

Still undaunted, he sailed to St. Brelard's Bay,
where he himself remained, despatching several
of his vessels to threaten a descent at various
parts of the island. At midnight the indefatigable
sailor had begun a fresh attempt. Four thousand
men in flat-bottomed boats made for the shore;
but Carteret was on the alert, and greeted them
with so heavy a fire that they were compelled
to return to their ships.

Baffled for the third time, Blake made new
plans. Leaving a squadron in St. Brelard's
Bay, he sailed back to his former position.
Carteret saw and followed rapidly; but he was
at a serious disadvantage. The ships sailed to
and fro without coming to an anchorage. The
unfortunate Royalists, wearied with toil, soaked
with rain, and half famished for want of food,
were obliged to march and countermarch till
they were half dead with fatigue.

Then when night fell, the admiral lowered his
boats and filled them with soldiers under Colonel
Haynes. It was a desperate undertaking, but it
was successful. Near the shore the men leaped
into the water and struggled gallantly to land.

Most of the garrison were asleep in the villages, but Carteret, faithful to his post, rushed down with his troopers and endeavoured to hurl the assailants into the sea.

For a short time success trembled in the balance; but Colonel Haynes, with splendid coolness, formed up his men and charged the dragoons with irresistible fury, driving them headlong from the ground. Following up his success, he had within three days forced the whole island, with the exception of Mount Orgueil and Elizabeth Castle, to submission.

Carteret's troops had lost hope, but their leader had no intention of yielding to despair. While Blake, leaving Colonel Haynes to invest Mount Orgueil, marched to St. Helier's, Carteret retired to Elizabeth Castle, which had been strongly fortified. Here, trusting to help from France, he believed himself secure; but his opponent, playing a hazardous game, brought up his frigates and began hammering at the castle walls.

Finding his guns of small effect against the massive fortress, Blake sent off post-haste to Plymouth for mortars, by means of which he inflicted such damage that the garrison became still further dispirited. To deepen their gloom, news arrived that Mount Orgueil had surrendered, and the besiegers were reinforced by Colonel Haynes and his victorious troopers.

But for two months longer Carteret, like the splendid soldier he was, held on grimly to his post, until his largest magazine was blown up and eighty brave fellows were buried in the ruins. Then Carteret reluctantly surrendered, and was permitted, with his principal officers, to retire to France.

With the fall of Jersey, Blake's work in this direction was finished. Prince Rupert was a fugitive; his fleet was destroyed; his strongholds were captured, and the hopes of the Royalists were finally crushed. From the moment when Sir George Carteret hoisted the white flag on Elizabeth Castle, the Stuart cause was lost, and the man who had blighted its prospects was Robert Blake.

CHAPTER VI.

A Fierce Struggle.

HONOURS and applause greeted Blake after his brilliant feats in the Channel, but the redoubtable sailor cared little for rewards or for popular acclamation. He had done what he considered his duty by weakening his country's foes, and he was content.

Another work now claimed his attention, and into this he immediately plunged with all his heart and soul. He had already accomplished much for the common sailor, but a great deal remained to be done, and thus it happened that the victorious fighter spent most of his waking hours in endeavouring to sweep away the abuses that had crept into the naval service.

He looked into everything, and wherever a

change could be made, he made it for the better. He listened patiently to the complaints of the humblest sailor, and, if a man had a just grievance, his admiral found means to remedy it. Well for England was it in the coming time of stress and danger that the ships with the red-cross flag sailed under the command of Robert Blake, who was trusted and adored by every man in the fleet.

A cloud was rising on the horizon—a cloud at first no bigger than a man's hand—which was to gather in volume until it burst and brought ruin and devastation to two countries.

The English Commonwealth had by this time made its position secure. True, it was not loved by foreign nations, but Blake had caused it to be respected and feared. He had taught both France and Spain a lesson, and there was no further danger to be apprehended from the exiled Stuarts. Strangely enough it was with Holland—a republic, and the chief Protestant state on the Continent— that trouble arose.

At that period the Dutch were a strong and powerful people. They owned colonies in all parts of the world ; their ships sailed on every sea ; their navy was superior to that of every other nation ; their sailors were brave, hardy, and daring ; their admirals were the most skilful sea- men afloat. It seemed as if the two nations ought to be the greatest friends ; as it was, they became the most deadly enemies.

Many things led to this strange state of affairs, but the most important was commercial jealousy. The English were growing stronger at sea; English merchant vessels were making longer and more successful voyages, and frequent disputes arose between the sailors of the two countries. Cromwell, anxious to encourage English trade, passed the famous Navigation Act, which dealt the Dutch a grievous blow.

Until that time Holland did the world's carrying trade. Almost all the produce of distant lands was transported from one country to another in Dutch ships. The Navigation Act declared that no goods should be imported into England except in English ships, or in vessels belonging to the country from which the goods were brought. Thus, at a stroke of the pen, Holland was deprived of a lucrative business, and, quite naturally, the Dutch were furious.

The quarrel grew more and more bitter, and the passions of the two peoples waxed to white heat, when the English Commonwealth resolved to revive an ancient custom. From very early times the English rulers had claimed the sovereignty of the narrow seas, and, as a token of supremacy, had ordered that all foreign vessels sailing thereon should strike their flag to any English warship. This order the Parliament now determined to enforce, and, as might have been expected, their resolution hastened the war.

An English commodore, falling in with a Dutch fleet, requested the admiral to lower his flag: the Dutchman haughtily refused, whereupon the English ships opened fire and compelled him to do so. When this startling news reached

Holland, the people were wild for war; a fleet was hastily fitted out, and the veteran Van Tromp, a magnificent sailor and courageous fighter, was appointed to the command, with instructions to mete out heavy punishment to the islanders who had insulted his country's flag.

There had been no declaration of war, when, one morning, word was brought to Blake that Van Tromp with a powerful fleet had appeared off Dover. In time of danger the English admiral always played his boldest part, and, without delay, he sailed to meet the enemy. At his approach Van Tromp retired, but he kept his flag flying. Blake had only fifteen ships with which to oppose forty-two; but he sent off a swift sailer to his lieutenant, Admiral Bourne, to bring up his eight vessels immediately. Then he put himself in fighting trim, and the battle began by a broadside from Van Tromp's ship into the *James,* commanded by Blake.

The English admiral did not know much about naval strategy, but, like Nelson in after years, he thought there could be little wrong if every ship tackled an enemy; so, in spite of the odds against him, he bore down on the foe. His own ship, the *James,* was in the thick of the fight and suffered fearfully. Cannon-ball after cannon-ball crashed into her sides; her masts were shot through, and her rigging hung in shreds. Blake ought to have been beaten, but he did not know that; so he thundered away with his guns while his men fell fast around him.

Towards nightfall, when the contest raged its

fiercest, a tremendous cheer arose from the crews of the sore-beset English vessels : they had caught the sound of fresh firing, and knew that the gallant Bourne was bearing down with crowded sail to their assistance.   His arrival turned the scale ; the Dutch, already severely handled, withdrew slowly, and when morning dawned not a hostile vessel— with the exception of two that had been captured —was in sight.

Even after this battle attempts were made to bring about a peaceable understanding between the two nations ; but, meanwhile, on the seas hostilities continued, and before long the English fleet had swept nearly half a hundred rich and valuable prizes into the Thames.   The Dutch were thunderstruck ; they could no longer use the Straits, but were forced to trust their costly cargoes on the long and dangerous northern route. To their intense astonishment and anger they discovered that they were no longer the masters of the narrow seas.

Finding that Van Tromp still lay in the Texel, Blake sailed North, where six hundred Dutch smacks, protected by twelve warships, were engaged in the herring fishery. The English Government claimed that the Dutch had no right to fish off the Scottish coasts, and Blake went to put a stop to it. He did not attain his object without a severe struggle.

The Dutch squadron, although hopelessly out-numbered, fought with the most gallant intrepidity for more than three hours, by which time three of the ships had been sunk and the remainder captured. Then Blake, having, as a mark of authority, exacted a tithe of the fish, sent the men to their homes, with the intimation that they were never to return without the permission of the English Government.

Meanwhile, Van Tromp had sailed for England, but, having been forced back by rough weather, he convoyed the Dutch merchant vessels on the first part of their long voyage and then returned to look for his enemy. The rival fleets met near the Orkneys, but a violent storm suddenly arose and dispersed the vessels.

So seriously was the Dutch fleet damaged that Van Tromp was forced to put back to Holland, having lost all his fireships and more than one of his frigates and cruisers. The English had escaped more lightly, and were able to chase their foe until the scattered ships found shelter in the ports of their country.

Blake had a greater courage than that of a mere fighting-man ; whatever he felt to be right, that he did without waiting for orders from the Parliament. This was shown in a striking manner soon after his return from the North. Dunkirk was at that time besieged by the Archduke Leopold, and Blake heard that the French had collected a fleet in the harbour of Calais, which was to sail to the relief of the beleaguered town.

Now, it was not to the interests of our country that Dunkirk should fall into the hands of the French. This Blake knew ; so without hesitation he crossed the Channel, fell on the French, captured almost the whole fleet, and returned triumphantly to Dover with his prize. Then, gathering his ships around him, he once more set sail to seek the Dutch.

Van Tromp's disaster in the North had sorely shaken the nerves of the Hollanders. With base ingratitude they turned upon the veteran who had fought for them so often and so victoriously, and the old man, heart-broken by this undeserved and cruel treatment, resigned his command. De Witt took his place, and with him sailed De Ruyter, probably the finest Dutch sailor who ever stepped on board a ship.

The English found their enemy off the North Foreland, and caught them in an unprepared state. The Dutch sailors did not want De Witt; they were angry at the scurvy treatment meted out to their veteran chief, and were unwilling to obey the commands of the new leader. De Ruyter wisely advised a retreat, but his superior would not listen to him; and very soon Blake, with his usual impetuosity, was bearing down upon them, accompanied by every English vessel that could keep the pace.

The battle opened with a heavy cannonade at short distance, and the havoc on both sides was frightful. The Dutch fell back, but they fell back fighting with the valour and obstinacy they had ever shown. De Witt fought with a courage and daring that roused even the most discontented of his men to admiration. He perilled his life a hundred times in the desperate endeavour to win a victory, but he could make no impression on

"The havoc on both sides was frightful."

the rough sea-dogs opposed to him. De Ruyter, too, did all that man could do. He carried his ship into the thickest of the action, and kept his flag flying to the last, though his decks were swept by the murderous missiles; his sails were ploughed through and through; his rigging was cut into shreds and patches, and his ship, riddled by shot, could barely float.

The coming of night put an end to the contest, but the English sailors had short time for repose. Throughout the hours of darkness they were hard at work repairing the damage and getting ready for a renewal of the conflict; their hearts cheered by the knowledge that thus far they had been the victors in the struggle. Two of the Dutch ships had been sunk; two others had been boarded, and captured with the whole of their officers and crews. The men toiled unceasingly at their labours, and, as soon as dawn shed a pale light over the sea, they once more bore toward the enemy.

De Witt, undaunted by the severe handling of the previous day, was eager to renew the battle, but was overruled. De Ruyter pointed out that the fleet was scattered, and that most of the ships were in no condition for further hard pounding. Better, he urged, to bear away for the Dutch coast, to reunite the vessels and to repair the mischief already done, than to sacrifice the fleet in a hopeless attempt to change defeat into victory.

Very reluctantly De Witt acknowledged the wisdom of this advice, and hoisted the signal for his vessels to make all sail for Holland.

The English hung on their track like sleuth-hounds, but in their disabled condition their progress was slow; and thus the two crippled fleets—hunted and hunters—crossed the Channel, until the Dutchmen fortunately found safety in the shallow waters off their coasts.

Very soon all England rang with news of the decisive victory, and the national joy was unbounded. The war was thought to be finished, and every one spoke in the highest terms of the daring admiral and his equally daring men, who had humbled the power of the greatest naval nation in the world. At the height of their rejoicings our forefathers considered the question of supremacy was finally settled, and that henceforth England—thanks mainly to Robert Blake—was Mistress of the Seas.

CHAPTER VII.

The Three Days' Fight.

IN our last chapter, we saw how scurvily the veteran Tromp was treated by the unthinking portion of his countrymen when he returned from the North with a shattered and disorganised fleet: a similar fate now befell the unfortunate De Witt. The news of his defeat roused the Hollanders to fury, and they cast down their new idol with as scant justice as they had their previous one. That the English were really their match on the high seas they could not,

and would not believe, attributing their defeat to
every reason but the right one.

The unexpectedness of the blow had disordered
their judgment, but it had not daunted their
energy nor lessened their courage. Their cry
was for more ships, more men, more ammunition
—and another stroke at the presuming islanders.
And in their fierce desire for vengeance they
sought out the brave old man whom they had
stripped of power, and placed him upon his
former pedestal.

The veteran seaman, who, more than any one,
had raised the Dutch navy to the pinnacle of
fame, was restored to his office, and with true
patriotism he put away from him the bitter
memory of past insults, and consented to lead
the ships of his country once more into action.
With him went, as second in command, the
chivalrous De Ruyter, a sailor fitting to rank in
naval genius and daring with Tromp himself.

Realising how stern the struggle was likely
to become, the Dutch endeavoured to secure an
ally in the King of Denmark, who, without
joining them openly, managed to do them a good
turn by keeping a number of English merchant
vessels, laden with hemp and tar, cooped up in
the Baltic. These stores were of the utmost
value to the fleet, and more than one attempt was
made to obtain possession of the ships, but the
Danish king trumped up various excuses in order
to detain them.

Meanwhile, the English Parliament was not
idle. At Blake's own request, Colonel Deane

and General Monk were appointed as his colleagues; fresh ships were built, damaged ones were repaired, and extra sailors were drafted into them. Left to themselves, the English Government would probably have considered all danger over; but Blake knew the Dutchmen better, although even he did not give them full credit for the feverish zeal and activity which they showed in getting ready for a renewal of the conflict.

The winter season approached, and Blake despatched his vessels to their various stations. Under his own immediate command were nearly forty warships and frigates, with which he cruised in the Channel. In those days a naval campaign during the storms of winter was almost unthought of, and the English admiral seems to have had the idea that there would be no further fighting till the spring. But in this he was reckoning without Tromp.

That brave veteran had flung himself into the work with the fire and energy of a headstrong and hot-headed youth. He was determined to retrieve his laurels, and by one swift, decisive blow to regain for his country her empire over the seas. Day and night, every port in Holland resounded with the clang of hammers, as skilled and vigorous shipwrights toiled with unflagging zeal to build and fit out a mighty armament. Fishermen from the north; sailors who in merchant vessels had ploughed the oceans in the far-off East; soldiers who burned to wipe out the recent defeats—all held themselves in readiness.

It might almost be said that the whole nation had thrown itself into the task of fashioning an invincible fleet.

And thus it happened that, one dark day in December, the lookout man on the *Triumph,* Blake's flagship, announced the approach of a vast armament. And then presently the crews of the English squadron saw the Channel, midway between Calais and Dover, studded with a hundred warships and frigates led by the indomitable Van Tromp. The situation was critical, but the English sailors had perfect confidence in their beloved admiral and refused to be discouraged.

Meanwhile, Blake had summed up the chances and had arrived at his decision. There was still time to withdraw; but such a course would leave the English shores exposed to the victorious enemy, and that was not to be thought of. His task was to guard the coast, and guard it he would. The odds against him were overwhelming; his squadron might be crushed, but before that time arrived it would at least have crippled the opposing fleet. If necessary, it must be sacrificed for the safety of the country. Like most of our successful admirals, Blake held strongly that it was the business of English ships to fight.

Van Tromp watched eagerly from the quarterdeck of the *Brederode,* and endeavoured to gain an advantageous position. The sun went down, leaving the fleets much as they had been, and with the coming of another dawn the manœuvres were resumed. Thus the morning passed, and by the afternoon the two fleets were off the Naze in Essex. Then Van Tromp made his dash, bearing down on the *Triumph,* but, missing the admiral's ship, he ran against the *Garland,* a vessel of forty-eight guns. It was like a fight between a giant and a dwarf, but the sailors of the *Garland* stood up with unparalleled bravery to their huge antagonist.

The heavy cannon-balls crashed into their ship; showers of bullets rattled down on the men at the guns; lusty Dutchmen, cutlass in hand, stood waiting, impatient to spring on the deck and overwhelm the crew by sheer force of numbers. Blake was ahead, making a desperate fight in the very midst of the hostile fleet; but the *Garland* was not left unfriended. Not far away was the little trading - vessel called the *Bonaventure,* mounted with only thirty guns, but carrying a brave captain and a gallant crew. Seeing their comrades' distress, they bore down with a rousing cheer to the fray, placing the *Brederode* between two fires.

The odds were barely equal even now, but the plucky pair held on like grim death, receiving and returning numerous broadsides. Then Evertz, the Dutch vice-admiral, seeing the awkward position of his chief, forced a way to the spot, and the two English ships were soon in a sorry plight. The *Garland* carried two hundred men; of these, sixty—including the captain and numerous officers—were killed, nearly a hundred badly hurt, and the survivors were too few to work the guns

and sail the ship. The *Bonaventure* was no better
off, and at last the triumphant Dutchmen leaped
with a shout on to the vessels' decks and bore
down all opposition.

Meanwhile, the remainder of the squadron had
maintained the fight against odds with equal
stubbornness and bravery till the darkness of
night began to fall. Then only did the English
admiral learn of the loss of his two vessels.
Instantly, in spite of weariness and fatigue, he
plunged anew into the conflict, making a splendid
effort to reach the *Brederode* and recapture the
prizes. His magnificent daring almost involved
him in destruction: ship after ship from the
Dutch fleet crossed his line, until he was ringed
round by foes.

The good old *Triumph,* the target for a hundred
guns, became a perfect wreck. Her sails and
masts were shot away; her hull was riddled like
a sieve. Band after band of excited Dutchmen
jumped on to her decks, only to be hurled back
to their own vessels or flung headlong into the
ravening sea. Then the little *Sapphire* and the
warship *Vanguard* pushed forward to their leader's
help, and Blake held his own till night put an
end to the conflict.

Slowly, very slowly, Robert Blake, beaten for
the first and last time in his career, fell back to
the Thames, leaving the Dutch to enjoy their
hardly-won triumph. But this defeat cast not a
shadow of discredit upon the admiral, and, when
he offered to resign his high office, Parliament
would not hear of it. The whole nation trusted

him as fully as ever, and knew that no man could have done more to preserve the national honour and the safety of his country.

Always open and straightforward, Blake asserted that, in spite of the undoubted bravery displayed by a portion of his fleet, some of his captains, either through treachery or cowardice, had failed to do their best, and three officers were despatched from London to make a searching and independent examination of the charges. As a result, several captains were deprived of their command, and among them was the admiral's brother Benjamin, to whom he was devotedly attached. But with Blake, duty was ever foremost, and he dealt out the same punishment to his brother as was accorded to the others.

Tromp, exulting in his victory, meanwhile cruised about, master of the Channel; but the English leader speedily collected a large fleet, and, with Admirals Penn and Lawson, and twelve hundred soldiers under Deane and Monk, went forth to seek the foe.

On February 18, 1653, the Dutch fleet was sighted convoying a vast number of merchant vessels. Tromp might have taken them home in safety, but, instead, he left them to look on while he engaged and destroyed the English fleet. His intention was to strike and crush the vanguard before the main body could arrive.

Blake, as usual, carried his ship into the foremost of the battle, and the Three Days' Fight began with a spirited engagement between the two admirals. Never, perhaps, within the knowledge of man had such a fearful conflict been waged. The sea was strewn with masts and cordage, and with wrecked ships. Here the lurid flames of a ship on fire lit up the darkness; there a loud explosion was heard, and the air for a moment was thick with the bodies of men; in another quarter some noble vessel, riddled with shot, heeled over and sank, carrying her crew to the depths below.

Both sides fought with heroic bravery, and the deeds of the English were matched by those of the Dutch. Van Tromp, De Ruyter, and Vice-Admiral Evertz led their men with conspicuous courage, and the people over in Holland had no cause to be ashamed of their brave sailors—though, when darkness fell, eight of their warships had been captured or destroyed. Several English vessels, too, had been taken, though all except one were recaptured.

Blake had received a wound in the thigh, but paid no heed to his hurt, directing all his energies to sending his wounded to the hospitals that had been prepared for them ashore, and to repairing the damages his ships had suffered.

The next day Tromp endeavoured to sail off with his convoy, but the English, giving him no rest, followed hard behind, until at length Tromp, bidding his merchant vessels seek their own safety, turned fiercely at bay. Again above the seething waves the din of battle was heard, and the fierce cries of angry men mingled with the heavy booming of cannon. Once more the gallant De Ruyter strained every nerve to wrest a victory, but the fortune of war went steadily against him, and by nightfall five more warships had been sunk or captured.

These two defeats broke the Dutch power. Several captains, pleading want of powder, told Tromp they could fight no longer, and he was forced to send them away with orders to join and protect the traders. Tromp could have had no hope of winning on the third day, but the old sailor stuck nobly to his post, ready to sacrifice himself for the protection of his convoy. But Blake, while continuing the fight, despatched his swiftest frigates in pursuit of the flying traders, some fifty of which fell into his hands.

Thus, in a confused, straggling crowd, the two fleets crossed the Channel, and Van Tromp anchored his battered vessels some four miles from Calais. Confident that he had his wily antagonist trapped at last, Blake cast his anchors and waited for the dawn; but the Dutch admiral was a superb seaman, and in the darkness he slipped past his vigilant foe, carrying the remnant of his fleet safely into the harbours of his native land.

CHAPTER VIII.

A Crushing Blow.

THE news of the decisive victory was received with unbounded enthusiasm in England; joy-bells rang, thanks and rewards were showered on the successful leaders, and provision was made for the support of the widows and orphans of the unfortunate sailors who had fallen in the conflict.

Blake, careless of applause and indifferent to honours, remained with the fleet, tending his wounded men, repairing his ships, and putting everything in trim to continue the war. He knew how severely the Dutch had been handled, but he knew, too, there were stout-hearted men among them who would never willingly acknowledge defeat. So he went on with his work, and, after paying a hasty visit to the Dutch coast, sailed away north with a small squadron, leaving his colleagues, Deane and Monk, to return to the Downs.

While Blake sailed north, important events were happening in England. Since the execution of Charles I., the government of the country had been carried on by a Council of State; but the real power had gradually fallen into the hands of Oliver Cromwell, who, in April 1653, dismissed the famous Long Parliament.

This is not the place to discuss whether Cromwell acted rightly or wrongly, but people who knew Blake well wondered how he would receive the news. He was a frank, outspoken republican, believing that the people should be ruled by a Parliament elected freely by themselves. He was a popular man, too, with great power in the country, and unbounded influence at sea. Idolised as he was by the sailors, there can be little doubt that, had he given the word, they would have refused allegiance to the new order of things, and thus probably have brought disaster on the country.

But Blake did not give the word. He was patriot enough to place country above personal opinion, and he knew that England required the loyal service of every single citizen.

"It is not for us to mind affairs of state," he declared, in a memorable speech to his captains, "but to keep foreigners from fooling us."

Well for England was it that he took this resolution, for very soon news came speeding north that Tromp and De Ruyter were again at sea and threatening Dover. Instantly Blake set sail, driving hard and fast on a southern course, eager to reach the scene of action. And while the sea-king, with every sail outspread to catch the breeze, is speeding on his way, let us see what had happened elsewhere.

Cromwell's action had inspired the Dutch with fresh hope. Believing that some of the English would not fight against them, they sailed from Holland, captured several traders, and fired on the coast towns. But their expectation that any of the English sailors would refuse to obey orders, was rudely shattered; Deane and Monk, Penn and Lawson collected their ships and moved out to meet the foe. De Ruyter and Lawson were the first to engage, but the others closed up, and the battle became general.

General Deane, on board the *Resolution,* was slain by almost the first shot, but George Monk —"Honest George," as the people called him— covered the body with his cloak, so that the men

might not be discouraged by the fall of a trusted
leader, and continued fighting with his usual
coolness and intrepidity. All day the battle raged
with extraordinary fury, and, when darkness fell
neither fleet could claim the victory.

That night both sides were busy in repairing
the damage done to spars and rigging, and while
the English toiled, they were asking one question
—Did Blake know? They were under the command of splendid officers, but they missed the
presence of the old sea-king who had led them
so often to victory. They knew that messengers
had ridden fast and furiously to him with the
news—but had they found him? They did not
ask what he would do, because they knew—but
had he heard?

Slowly the night passed; dawn broke gray over
the troubled sea; the sun rose, and thousands of
anxious eyes scanned the horizon for a sight of
the veteran's sails. Tromp did not expect him,
and spent the morning in obtaining a favourable
position. About noon the heavy guns began a
tremendous cannonade. Both sides fought stubbornly, and the result of the battle still hung in
the balance, when about two o'clock in the afternoon the roar of fresh artillery was heard in the
rear of the Dutch fleet.

Hurrah! Blake had come! The pulses of the
sailors beat more swiftly as they realised that
their leader was with them. And as they gazed,
a single ship, belching fire from port and star-
board, was observed clearing a passage through
the Dutch fleet. It was the first of Blake's

squadron, and was led by the admiral's nephew and namesake.

This arrival placed the enemy in a hopeless position, but, even so, they made a determined effort to retrieve the fortunes of the day. De Witt, who was now serving under Tromp, and the chivalrous De Ruyter exposed themselves with matchless bravery, but the most reckless fighter in the two fleets was Van Tromp himself. Even after this lapse of time, our hearts go out to this gallant enemy as we picture him in the heat and stress of the fight absolutely refusing to acknowledge defeat, but driving the battered old *Brederode* into the midst of the fray.

He brought his vessel alongside Penn's ship, the *James*, and, with shouts of defiance, the Dutchmen boarded their opponent. After a fierce strife they were driven back, and the fight was transferred to the *Brederode's* deck. The capture of the Dutch flagship appeared certain; but the admiral was a man of iron will, and, rather than be taken, he threw a burning brand into the powder magazine. Instantly a fearful explosion occurred; the upper deck was blown into the air, and every English boarder perished.

It was the last act in the tragedy; the Dutch captains believed their admiral was dead, and though in a swift frigate he sailed from ship to ship, showing himself to the crews, he was unable any longer to prevent the dispersal of his fleet. Even then, however, his marvellous seamanship came to the rescue, and in spite of a hot pursuit he carried the greater portion of his fleet into

"Threw a burning brand into the magazine."

s^fety. But, for a time at least, the Dutch naval power was crushed.

Blake had now a tedious and dreary task before him. Having sent home his wounded men and the captured ships, he selected the best of his vessels with which to blockade the coasts of Holland and to destroy the Dutch trade. He had little to fear from the remnant of the Dutch navy, but he had many difficulties to contend with in his own squadron.

His ships, even the soundest, were in a pitiable condition ; he was short of men ; powder and shot were running low ; there was a lack of fresh water, and he had not sufficient provisions. The food on board was wretched stuff, and in consequence of this and of the absence of necessary clothing, disease broke out. The sick wards were crowded with disabled sailors, numbers of whom died ; and the admiral himself, suffering from the old wound in his leg, and from anxiety for his men, steadily grew worse.

But, hampered as he was, Blake remained at his post, keeping Tromp shut up, and capturing the Dutch traders as they returned from distant lands laden with valuable cargoes. Now and again he received a welcome addition to his stores, but the prospect was gloomy in the extreme, and, had the Dutch been in a condition to make one supreme effort, the English might have been hard put to it to hold their own.

Still the great hearted leader knew neither fear nor doubt. Week after week his ships sailed the seas in triumph, snapping up every Dutch trader

whose captain had either the temerity or ill-
fortune to pass their way. But though nothing
could sap Blake's wonderful courage, his strength
was rapidly declining. The pain of his wound
increased, anxiety for the welfare of his crews
harassed his spirits, and it became evident even
to himself that the time had come when he must
lay aside his command.

Sorrowfully the ships stood over to England,
and the famous commander, weak as a child, was
carried ashore, to the intense regret of every man
on board. But even in his extreme weakness he
had not forgotten the need of his country. He
had entrusted his plans to Monk, Penn, and
Lawson, and, while lying on his bed of sickness,
he had the satisfaction of knowing that the fleet
was in capable hands.

As soon as the English had departed from the
shores of Holland, Van Tromp, De Ruyter, and
Evertz came out from their hiding-places; but
Blake had already broken their power, and it
only remained for his colleagues to deal the final
stroke. For the last time in this stubborn war
the hostile fleets met in battle array; it was
already dark when the contest began, and night
soon put a stop to the desultory fighting. The
next day was dark and stormy, and the vessels
were enveloped in so thick a haze that nothing
could be done.

Monk was in command of the English fleet, and,
determined to bring the long struggle to a decisive
conclusion, he ordered his captains to give no
quarter, and to make no prizes, but to sink and

destroy every captured ship. On the third day
the battle raged furiously, and once more the
Dutch were compelled to own that they had met
their masters. In vain Van Tromp displayed the
most skilful seamanship, and the most stubborn
valour ; in vain De Ruyter and Evertz encouraged
their men by unexampled bravery ; steadily and
surely the battle went against them.

And then occurred a crowning mishap! A
musket-ball pierced the heart of the gallant Van
Tromp, and the intrepid Dutch admiral, than
whom no braver man had ever commanded a fleet,
fell dead. It would have been a heavy blow at
any time : at that moment it meant destruction for
the Dutch navy. Conscious of defeat which they
could not avert, many of his captains fled, with
the English in swift pursuit dealing out death
with every discharge of their heavy guns. Thirty
ships were destroyed, and most of their crews
perished, while the vessels that escaped were
so beaten and pounded as to be almost unfit for
further service.

The news of this last victory filled England
with rejoicing. Golden chains and medals were
bestowed on the successful admirals, and extra
wages were granted to the seamen who had taken
part in the action. A magnificent banquet was
given by the City of London to celebrate the
victory, and while the guests sat at table Oliver
Cromwell himself placed the golden chain round
Monk's neck.

Crushed by the calamity that had befallen them,
the Dutch hastened to sue for peace. The terms

which the English Government imposed were far from light. Compensation was demanded and obtained for the English traders who had suffered during the war, and for the East India Company, and the royal exiles were banished from Holland. But probably what our brave antagonists felt most was having to pay honour to the English flag in the narrow seas. For the time, however, they dared not refuse ; their losses had been enormous, and they were in no condition to hold out against the victors.

Meanwhile, the one man who had paved the way to victory, not only by his skill and daring, but by his humane treatment of his men and by his incessant toil, lay on a bed of sickness, knowing little of the tumultuous applause of his country, or of the praises of himself which were in all men's mouths.

CHAPTER IX.

A Brilliant Campaign.

UNTIL the December of 1653, Robert Blake remained on shore, prostrated at first by fever, dropsy, and scurvy. But his iron constitution and simple habits enabled him to overcome these diseases, and by degrees he recovered a portion of his former strength and vigour, though his wound had left him lame for life.

This period, however, was not one of idleness : the Government recognised the value of his advice, and even while he lay ill he was consulted on every important project. He was still the admiral-in-chief, and, when his term of office expired, he was immediately re-elected to the important position. The Government and the country were well aware that it would be difficult to replace him.

In December 1653, he hoisted his flag on the *Swiftsure,* and, as the treaty with Holland was not yet settled, he stationed his ships to intercept any of the Dutch traders adventuring in the narrow seas. The conclusion of the treaty, however, left him at liberty to return, and, for a short time he was employed by the Government as a commissioner to inquire into the state of the churches.

Before long he was recalled from this peaceful service in order to superintend the fitting-out of a fresh fleet. At this time France and Spain were at war with each other. Both countries had shown keen hostility to the new English Government, though no outbreak of war had occurred. Now they began to ask themselves if Cromwell intended to use this new armament against either of them. Hitherto they had affected rather to despise the English, but circumstances had altered. Thanks mainly to Blake, England was now the undoubted Mistress of the Seas; her friendship was of immense value, her enmity something to be feared and dreaded.

Cromwell pushed on with his preparations and kept his own counsels. He was forging a tremendous weapon, but none could tell against whom he intended to use it. At length his plans were completed; a magnificent fleet, for those days, was collected and divided into two squadrons —one under Blake; the second under Admiral Penn, who had with him three thousand soldiers commanded by General Venables. The squadrons sailed from the Solent, with sealed orders, and Penn set his sails for the Atlantic.

Cromwell was not yet ready to show his hand, but Blake had sufficient work to occupy his time. Whatever view we may take of Cromwell's character, it must be admitted that he raised the power of England abroad; and when Blake, after a short stay in Cadiz harbour, appeared in the Mediterranean, more than one potentate began to tremble.

The first to feel the sea-king's power was the Grand Duke of Tuscany, who in former days had allowed Prince Rupert to sell a number of prizes in his territory. For this, Blake now claimed redress and demanded a sum of £60,000 as compensation. In vain the Grand Duke blustered and talked about his rights; Blake pointed his guns at the towers of Leghorn, and the Grand Duke, unable to resist such powerful arguments, yielded.

Rupert had sold some of his prizes in Roman ports also, and the Pope in his turn was compelled to pay a sum of money in reparation. Having thus asserted the might of England, Blake was busily preparing for a new expedition, but a violent storm put his ships in peril, and he himself, with many of his crew, was stricken with the plague. For a time he was too weak even to hold a pen ; but he gradually recovered, and, at the first approach of favourable weather, he set sail for Goletta.

The natives who lived on the shores of the Mediterranean were beginning to speak with awe of this quiet man with the iron will who carried the red-cross flag at the masthead of his ship, and to think that it might be dangerous to play tricks on English traders in the future. From port to port the news of his doings was noised, and men whispered to one another how even the most powerful princes were obliged to do what he wished. To their astonishment it became plain that these English must be taken into account after all.

Up to this time England had been represented in the Mediterranean by trading vessels alone, and their crews had often met with a far from pleasant reception. There were few friendly ports into which an English ship could run, and even now the famous sailor had to depend upon England for a large portion of his provisions.

But Blake had a special mission to perform, and he was not the man to be easily frightened by a few obstacles. At that time the Mussulman states on the north shores of Africa were nests of pirates. The men were strong, hardy, and lawless, and they made a living by plundering helpless merchantmen. Far worse than this, however, was their habit of seizing the crews and selling them into slavery. The sailors of all nations formed their prey, and they laughed alike at threats and pleadings.

They had some respect for the Dutch, but for
the English they cared nothing at all. England
was a strange country, far away, and these outlaws
of the Mediterranean knew no reason why they
should respect her flag. This was the lesson
Blake had resolved to teach them, and hitherto he
had been a stern master. The western nations of
Europe had learned something of the power of
England at sea, and he quite intended that these
ruthless pirates should learn something also.

His first visit was paid to the Dey of Tunis,
a warlike prince whose territory was defended
by the strong and well-manned fortresses of
Goletta and Porto Ferino. The Dey listened to
his visitor's demands, and agreed readily enough
to respect the English flag in future. But on
one point he was as stubborn as the English
admiral himself could be. Blake sternly insisted
that several English ships which had recently
been captured should be restored, and that all
English captives should be set free. The Dey
haughtily refused this request, and it was seen
that the only arguments he would recognise were
cannon-balls.

Blake blocked the harbour with his frigates,
and pushed in close to the shore in order to
examine the defences. The Dey had drawn up
his ships under the big guns of the castles, had
collected a fine army, and had lined the bay
with formidable batteries. The nut was evidently
a hard one to crack, and the English fleet was
in poor condition for the work. Bread and water
were both lacking; so, leaving a few frigates to

watch the harbour, the sea-king sailed away in order to obtain provisions.

The Dey laughed at this sudden ending, and concluded that his opponent had gone off through fear. He became more certain, when several weeks passed without the return of the English fleet. But on the 8th of March Blake re-appeared and pressed his demands anew. The Dey meanwhile had recovered his confidence; he refused every proposal, and would not even allow the sailors to obtain water.

"Tell the Dey," said Blake, "that God has given the benefit of water to all his creatures; and for men to deny it to each other is equally insolent and wicked."

The Dey, feeling safe in his defences, laughed.

"Here," said he, "are our castles of Goletta and Porto Ferino; do your worst, and do not think to frighten us with the mere sight of your grand fleet."

The challenge was promptly accepted—and, indeed, Blake could have done no other. The honour of England was at stake now, and when that was the case, the sea-king never stopped to count the cost.

"We judged it necessary," he wrote in his account of the business, "for the honour of the fleet, our nation, and religion, seeing they would not deal with us as friends, to make them feel us as enemies."

But the enterprise was not one to be lightly undertaken, and, in order to throw the enemy off their guard, Blake once more sailed away. The ruse was, to a certain extent, successful, and the pirates were led to believe that their position was impregnable. They were, however, soon to be undeceived.

Once more the English ships appeared in sight, but no more messages were sent on shore. The time for words had passed; the time for deeds had come. Silently, but with majestic sweep, the squadron rode into the harbour, the frigates leading the way. The pirates looked on in wonder as the stately ships came to their stations right in front of the fortresses. Such an act of daring had rarely been witnessed.

Suddenly a gun from the shore belched forth its iron missiles, and a tremendous artillery duel began. For two long hours the storm lasted; the guns from the fortresses hurling a hail of iron into the vessels, and the vessels replying with destructive broadsides that tore the breastworks to pieces and dismounted several of the heavy cannon.

But Blake had no intention of trusting solely to his guns. He had another plan in his head— a plan so full of peril that only complete confidence in the bravery of his sailors justified him in attempting it. Under cover of the dense smoke, the long-boats were lowered and manned by picked crews. John Stoaks, the captain of the *St. George,* led them, and in face of a hot and galling fire they rowed swiftly but steadily toward the pirate ships.

The gunners on shore fired volley after volley, but no danger could daunt those steady rowers.

On they went until their boats were alongside
the pirate warships ; then, ceasing to pull, they
flung lighted brands into the huge vessels until
all were completely enveloped in flames. They
burned furiously, and sea and sky were lit up
by the red glare. In vain the pirates rushed
on to the burning decks, in the endeavour to
quench the blaze. Blake's guns were trained
on the doomed vessels, and before long the
once dreaded fleet was but a cluster of charred
fragments.

The havoc on shore was almost as complete.
The batteries were silenced : many of the guns
were overturned and smashed ; the walls of the
fortresses were rent and gaping ; the Dey's stronghold lay open to a vigorous assault. But that
savage ruler had already taken his lesson to
heart, and Blake sailed off in triumph to Tripoli.
The ruler there, dazed by what had happened
at Tunis, greeted him with every token of respect
and agreed to all his demands.

The Mussulmans were then at war with Venice,
and, when Blake entered the Adriatic, the Venetians
crowded joyfully to welcome him. They, too,
were beginning to understand how much henceforth the red-cross flag would mean in the
waters of the Mediterranean.

Blake had still to visit Algiers, another strong
nest of pirates ; but his fame had gone before him,
and the Dey was shrewd enough to speak in
humble tones and to make the fairest promises
for the future. Accordingly, Blake agreed to pay
a moderate sum for the freedom of all the English

slaves in Algiers, and numbers of poor fellows, who had long abandoned all hope of escape from their wretched condition, were thus restored to liberty.

The English ships were still lying in the harbour, when an incident occurred which showed in the strongest light the noble nature of the sailors who formed their crews. Several men were suddenly seen swimming towards the vessels, while a number of boats manned by Moors followed in swift pursuit. The swimmers were runaway Dutch slaves, who begged the sailors to rescue them from their masters. Without hesitation the gallant Jack Tars helped them into the ships and kept the Moors off.

Thereupon the Dey sent a message to the admiral, pointing out that nothing about the Dutch sailors was in the bargain and asking that they should be sent back. Such a proceeding could not be thought of, and in order to make a way out of the difficulty, an Englishman suggested they should be ransomed. So Blake and his officers opened a subscription, and every sailor in the fleet gave up a dollar of his pay to buy the release of the Dutch slaves.

Blake's campaign in the Mediterranean was a brilliant success, and we are proud of it; but we are prouder still of the humane and unselfish action performed by these rough sea-dogs who sailed under his flag.

"The swimmers were runaway Dutch slaves."

CHAPTER X.

The Silver Fleet.

IT will be remembered that when Blake began his cruise in the Mediterranean, a formidable fleet under Penn had steered its course, under sealed orders, into the Atlantic. Even Penn, at the moment of starting, did not know what he was to be called upon to do; but by this time the secret was out, for news had reached Europe that Penn had made a descent on the Spanish settlement of Hispaniola.

As a matter of fact, Cromwell had from the first resolved upon a war with Spain, with which country England always had cause for disagreement. The two states were sharply divided on the questions of religion and trade. The Spaniards were strict Roman Catholics, and would tolerate no form of religion but their own; the English, as a nation, were decided Protestants, and were frequently roused to fury by tales of Spanish cruelty.

Then, again, Spain flatly refused to open her American ports to commerce, and prevented English traders from visiting the West Indies. An English vessel attempting to trade on the Spanish Main, was regarded as a pirate and treated accordingly. Cromwell resolved that this state of things should be altered. To us it appears strange that he should strike a blow without any declaration of war; the act seems to savour somewhat of hitting below the belt, but in those days such ideas did not exist.

Therefore Penn was despatched on his secret expedition, and in due time Blake received orders to repass the Straits of Gibraltar. As war had not yet been declared, he called in at Malaga for water, where a striking incident occurred. Some of his men, while on shore, made fun of a Catholic procession, which so angered one of the priests that he called on the people to avenge the insult offered to their religion. A fierce fight followed, and the sailors, unable to make headway against the heavy odds, were driven pell-mell to their ships, where they complained to Blake of their ill-treatment.

The admiral took prompt action, and demanded that the priest should be given up to him. The governor of the town refused, saying that he had no power over the clergy; but Blake insisted.

"If he be not on board the *St. George* within three hours," said he sternly, "I will burn your city to the ground."

The threat was one not to be lightly disregarded, and within the time named the priest had arrived on board. Then the admiral heard both sides of the story and delivered judgment. The sailors, he said, had behaved badly, and, had their conduct been reported to him, they should have been severely punished; but he could not allow others to punish them. With this warning he set the priest at liberty, to the intense astonishment of the citizens.

From Malaga the fleet sailed to Cadiz Bay, where it remained for a short time, and almost immediately after its departure arrived the news of Penn's doings in the West Indies. The expedition had met with but partial success; it had, indeed, failed miserably in Hispaniola, but had afterwards succeeded in capturing the fine island of Jamaica.

These tidings naturally brought on open war between the two countries. Philip of Spain was beside himself with anger, and he entered upon the campaign with the fixed determination to crush England's fast-rising power. Blake kept the sea, waiting for the Spanish Silver Fleet which was expected from America in the course of a few weeks. But the Silver Fleet did not come, and Philip's warships still remained snug in harbour. At length the Spanish merchants fitted out a squadron at their own expense, but, chiefly by reason of foggy weather and contrary winds, no battle between the hostile forces took place.

Although the blockading of Cadiz caused the Spaniards serious loss, yet as time passed the position of their enemies became more and more dangerous. Several of the English vessels were leaky and in bad repair; food was scarce; fresh vegetables could not be obtained; the biscuits were full of weevils; the meat had to be boiled in salt water, and what fresh water remained for drinking purposes was foul and stinking. Under these conditions there is little cause for surprise that numbers of men fell seriously ill, and that the dreadful disease of scurvy carried off numerous victims.

The admiral was attacked, and to his bodily weakness was added the heavy burden of responsibility. Yet he clung obstinately to his post, until, realising that no help was likely to be received from England, and feeling sure that the famous fleet had not left America, he turned the prows of his vessels homeward. Ill and worn-out by toil and privation, he would gladly have laid down his command; but the country needed his services, and he was far too unselfish to place his own interests first.

With all the energy he could command, he busied himself in refitting the ships and getting ready for the fresh enterprise. Before setting sail again he asked to be supplied with a colleague, and Cromwell sent to him a brilliant young soldier named Montagu.

One other thing he did, which shows whither at this time the thoughts of the aged admiral tended. A few days before the expedition started, he wrote his will, in which he directed that a hundred pounds should be set aside for the poor people of Bridgwater. There can be little doubt that the old sea-king already began to see the shadow of the approaching end. But we may be sure he maintained a stout heart, though probably he gazed with wistful eyes at the white cliffs of his native land, which it was fated he should never see again.

Straight for Cadiz Bay he sailed; the Spanish ships were again shut in, and could offer no aid if the Silver Fleet made its appearance. The English vessels took up their allotted positions and began the dreary task of patrolling the sea.

But Blake was suddenly diverted from his task by strange news from Lisbon. King John of Portugal had refused to sign the treaty he had made with England, and the English envoy had been murderously assaulted in the streets. Leaving a few frigates to watch Cadiz, Blake started in hot haste for the Portuguese capital. All his old fire and energy were displayed, and so much was he held in awe that the sight of his ships at the mouth of the Tagus was sufficient to ensure his commands being carried out.

Then returning to Cadiz harbour, he resumed his watch ; but the Spaniards would not venture forth, and nothing could be heard of the famous Silver Fleet. It was no easy matter to ride those dangerous seas, and on one occasion a terrible storm arose, scattering the vessels far and wide, tearing the sails to ribbons, smashing the boats, and snapping the cables asunder. Six of the ships were so damaged, and so evidently unsuitable for the rough service, that Blake sent them home.

A flying visit to Malaga was attended with complete success. The English ships rode into the harbour to punish a Sicilian galley, and one from Genoa, for having assisted the Spaniards. The two galleys attempted to escape, and in the confusion the Sicilian slipped away ; but the Genoese, severely damaged, was compelled to run back, when she was quickly set on fire and burned to the water's edge. Then the shore batteries opened a fierce cannonade, but a small party of resolute sailors rowed to the land in a long-boat, leaped ashore, and with the most amazing intrepidity actually spiked eight of the heaviest guns.

But the real object of the expedition seemed as far off as ever. The Silver Fleet had not yet put in an appearance; summer was rapidly passing; the stormy weather of autumn approached; bread was scarce, it was almost impossible to obtain water, and all the vessels sorely required overhauling.

By the beginning of September it was absolutely necessary to procure a fresh store of food and water; so the two admirals sailed for Portugal, leaving the valiant Captain Stayner, who had already greatly distinguished himself, to keep ward. It was well, from the English point of view, that Blake had left behind so able and trustworthy a lieutenant.

In the evening of September 8, 1656, four Spanish galleons and two Indiamen, laden with gold, silver, precious stones, and a costly general cargo from the Far West, appeared in sight. The Spanish commander, misled by false reports, believed that the English fleet had been driven off, and concluded that the vessels lying in front of the harbour belonged to his own country. In this belief, he actually hung out lights during the darkness and made no attempt to escape.

Daylight revealed how badly he had been deceived, but it was then too late to repair the mischief. A rough gale had scattered the English squadron; but three ships, including Stayner's, still remained together, and they immediately fell upon the galleons. The Spanish admiral escaped into Cadiz, but the rest were forced to fight. The battle was of the fiercest description, and it resulted in an almost complete destruction of the Spanish fleet—two of the vessels alone succeeding in reaching shelter.

The Spaniards fought with desperate valour, their vice-admiral especially defending his flag in the most heroic manner. But at last his gallant sailors were overpowered by numbers, and the English, after removing the prisoners, took out all the gold and silver, and then left the vessel, already enveloped in flames, to sink. In six hours fighting, the Spaniards had suffered a loss equal in money value to £2,000,000.

Before the tidings of this brilliant achievement reached England, the Government had recalled Montagu for the purpose of consulting with him; so Blake removed his flag to the *Swiftsure,* collected his prizes, and despatched a part of the fleet to England under the command of his young colleague. He himself remained, with the best of his ships, to harass the Spaniards, and to ruin their commerce.

Such was the penalty of fame! Had he been a less distinguished man, he might have returned, and ended his days peacefully in the old home of which in his later years he had seen so little. But England could not afford to lose his services, and the old sea-dog after watching the fast-receding sails of the homeward-bound vessels, turned his gaze steadily toward the Spanish harbour.

Meanwhile, England went wild with joy at the news of this fresh and striking success. Montagu was greeted with acclamation and richly rewarded; Captain Richard Stayner, the successful leader, became Sir Richard, and none could deny that he had earned his title. The booty he had captured from the ill-fated Spaniards was landed at Portsmouth, and thirty-eight wagons, guarded by escorts of soldiers, drew it to London.

Let us hope that, amidst the cheers and rejoicings, the people of England spared a kindly thought for the noble old man, who even then, stricken by illness though he was, continued to keep watch and ward for the sake of the country he loved so devotedly.

CHAPTER XI.

A Deed of Daring.

THE task which Blake had set himself was, in those days, one of unexampled difficulty, and there were few people who thought he would succeed. Most of his warships had returned home, and his squadron now consisted almost entirely of frigates. With these he intended to brave the wild storms and fierce tempests of the ocean for a whole winter.

The Spaniards laughed loudly at the idea, thinking his vessels would be hurled to destruction by the tempestuous gales which would assuredly come with the close of the year. But the days passed into weeks; October gave way to November, and never for a moment was the bay destitute of an English ship. Often the squadron was scattered by a tremendous gale, but always some vessel kept her station, while the others speedily returned.

It was a marvellous performance of seamanship and endurance, this keeping the seas during the memorable winter of 1656, and we may well be proud of the leader and his men who accomplished it. Soaked with rain, chilled by the bitter winds, wearied with incessant labour, they remained at their posts fighting the ocean and blockading the Spanish harbours at one and the same time.

Slowly the dark days crawled by; December came and went, and the opening of the New Year, 1657, found the sea still dotted by the battered English ships. In one of his letters home, Blake wrote: "Truly our fleet is generally in that condition, that it troubles me to think what the consequences may prove if such another storm, as we have had three or four lately, should overtake us before we have time and opportunity a little to repair. Our number of men is lessened through death and sickness, occasioned partly through the badness of victuals and the long continuance of poor men at sea. Therefore I desire that, if you intend us to stay out this summer, or any considerable part thereof, that you will forthwith send us a sufficient supply of able seamen."

No help was sent to him, but nevertheless the brave old admiral hung on doggedly with his damaged frigates, some of which were so short-handed that the crews could barely work them. The country might forget him, but as long as two planks would hold together he was determined that the red-cross flag should still wave triumphantly in the Spanish seas.

At last it seemed as if his patience was about to be rewarded. One day a letter reached him with the information that the second Silver Fleet had left America, but that on learning of the destruction of its predecessor it had run into Santa Cruz for safety. Blake at first felt inclined to doubt the truth of this report, which might have been circulated by the Spaniards for the express purpose of luring him from the Spanish coast; but later on the same news reached him through other channels, and then without further delay he decided on his action.

On the 13th of April he bore away with his whole fleet, bound on the most memorable enterprise ever recorded—till that period, at least—in the annals of naval warfare.

Santa Cruz was one of the most formidable strongholds in the world, and the commanders of the Silver Fleet felt confident that their vessels were in no danger from even the mightiest armaments. The harbour was of horse-shoe shape, defended at the entrance by a massive castle in which were mounted the heaviest cannon then cast; seven forts guarded the inner bay, and all these were connected by solid lines of earthworks.

In addition were the warships of the fleet, themselves a match for the finest squadron afloat. No wonder the Spaniards laughed when they heard the English were approaching; no wonder that Don Diego Diagues, the governor, exclaimed with a smile on his face, "Let Blake come if he dare."

But the English admiral was a man who, during his life, had dared many things, and when a swift frigate brought the certain news that the Silver Fleet lay in Santa Cruz harbour, his mind was instantly made up. For many weary months, ill in mind and body, he had sailed the tempestuous seas; he and his trusty men had endured untold hardships and privations, and now the prey they had waited for so long and looked for so anxiously was close at hand. Desperate as was the enterprise, we cannot wonder at the sea-king's decision to undertake it.

Rising from a sick-bed, he called his captains around him and explained his plans. It was impossible to bring off the stately galleons, but it was not impossible to destroy them. Such was the tenor of the admiral's words, and though some of the officers thought the feat impracticable, the old sea-dogs who had seconded their master in many a hazardous enterprise felt no doubts. With him to lead them they felt quite certain as to the result.

And so, in the early morning light, the sailors gathered together for prayers, and then, serene and confident, they prepared for their deadly work. To the gallant Stayner, who was now a vice-admiral, was entrusted the difficult task of destroying the galleons, while Blake himself attacked the castle and forts. With marvellous daring the vice-admiral led forward his squadron, and, though the Spaniards sent destructive broadsides crashing into his ships, he took up his appointed position.

Blake meanwhile drew the fire from the castle and the forts, and returned it with interest. His gunners were trained men who rarely wasted a shot. The Spaniards fought with splendid courage; every fort belched forth fire, and the marksmen behind the earthworks discharged volley after volley. But the bull-dogs had got their grip and could not be shaken off. Men fell fast, but, as one fell, another sprang to take the vacant place. It was a terrible game to play, but it was played to the end.

And while we record with pride the feats of our own sailors, let us not be unjust to a gallant foe. Don Diego proved himself an intrepid leader, and among his troops was no sign of cowardice or of wavering. But the English shot fell fast and furiously, uncovering or dismounting their guns and doing fearful execution. For four hours the battle between warships and forts raged, and then Blake perceived that the enemy were beaten. Leaving a few frigates to finish the work, he swiftly swung the rest of his ships round to the help of his able colleague.

All this time the dashing vice-admiral had been engaged in a life and death struggle. The Spanish vessels were heavier than his; they were better armed, better manned, and in a far better position. But Stayner was a sea-king, too, and Blake had not chosen him for nothing. His ship, the *Speaker,* was in the van, and he had, one might say, nailed his colours to the mast. Already two of the mighty galleons had sunk, and more than one of the others were in flames.

A rousing cheer went up from the toiling sailors as Blake approached in the flag-ship, and the fury of the cannonade redoubled. Still the Spaniards fought doggedly on, but now they could cherish no hope of victory. Vessel after vessel caught fire, until every craft in the harbour was enveloped in flames that could not be quenched. Royal galleon, majestic warship, humble trader—all shared the same fate; and for miles around the waters reflected the red glare. The destruction was complete, and of all that proud armament nothing was left but a few blackened keels and drifting spars.

Before the battle began Dan Diego had carried on shore the gold and silver, and precious stones; but an immense treasure in the shape of spices, silks, hides, and other valuable products of the Far West was burned, or buried in the depths of the ocean. The victory was the most complete in naval history, and, as soon as the battle ended, Blake set about withdrawing his vessels from their dangerous position. Strangely enough a sudden change of wind came to his aid, and, without the loss of a single ship, though the *Speaker* was hopelessly damaged, Blake sailed from the harbour where he had committed such fearful havoc.

Men stood aghast when they heard of the feat. Nothing to equal it had ever been done in any quarter of the globe. Even the English Royalists, who bitterly detested Blake's politics, could not repress a thrill of pride and exultation when the news reached Europe.

"Of all the desperate attempts that were ever made in the world against an enemy by sea," wrote one, "this of the noble Blake's is not inferior to any."

Clarendon, the trusted friend of the exiled Stuarts, and the gifted historian of the Civil War, wrote : "The whole action was so miraculous, that all men who knew the place concluded that no sober man, with what courage soever endued, would ever undertake it ; whilst the Spaniards comforted themselves with the belief that they were devils and not men who had destroyed them in such a manner."

The great body of the English people hailed the victory with the most enthusiastic rejoicing ; thanks were sent to the officers of the fleet by Parliament, and £500 were set aside with which to buy the admiral a jewel as a mark of honour. Cromwell himself wrote him a letter of congratulation on his wonderful achievements.

But, meanwhile, the victor at Santa Cruz had a melancholy task to perform, and the story affords one more proof of his rigid devotion to duty at whatever cost. One of the captains of the fleet was his brother Humphrey, and, after the battle, it was whispered about that he had been guilty of cowardice. The pitiful rumour reached the admiral, and, in spite of his love for his favourite brother, he ordered him to be tried by court-martial. In vain the officers begged him to spare himself this pain; in vain they endeavoured by every means in their power to shield the erring sailor. Blake was inflexible.

Always first and foremost in his mind was the honour of England, and nothing could excuse the man who had tarnished it. Humphrey was tried, and the charge being found proved, he was sent home and dismissed from the service. What it cost the brave old admiral to sign the judgment-sheet, who shall say?—but although even then on the brink of the grave, he never faltered in his resolution.

He might yet have returned to England in time to see the white cliffs once again, but he had one more task to fulfil before he laid down for ever the command with which his country had entrusted him. The Moors of Salee had long scoured the Mediterranean in swift-sailing boats; many a captured trader had been towed in triumph into their harbour, and numerous Christian slaves were still held in bondage. It was Blake's earnest desire to pay a visit to this pirate stronghold, and to force the robbers, at the cannon's mouth, to surrender their unhappy prisoners.

Once more came a parting of the ways. The old hero longed with passionate longing to draw his last breath in his quiet home; but duty pointed in the opposite direction, and, true to the principle which had guided him through life, he followed it. As it chanced, there was no need to fire a single shot. His fame had preceded him, and the men of Salee hastened to obey his every wish. They agreed to his terms, and, bringing out all their Christian captives, set them at liberty.

Then the veteran turned the prows of his vessels toward the loved land that he was to reach only in spirit. In all history there are few things more sad and affecting than the last home-coming of Robert Blake. He lay in his cabin, surrounded by his officers, dying. League by league the *St. George* swept on; the Lizard hove in sight; then the hills of Cornwall and at last the famous harbour at Plymouth.

The news of his coming had been noised abroad, and the shores were lined by dense crowds waiting to welcome the gallant leader. But alas! it was fated far otherwise! Even as the battered vessel entered the spacious harbour the soul of the hero passed away, and the joyous acclamations of the people were suddenly turned into sobs of grief and mourning.

Robert Blake was dead, and England had lost the finest seaman who ever flew the red-cross flag. They buried him in Westminster Abbey, and Roundhead and Cavalier joined in paying homage to the illustrious dead. Few men have ever done so much for England; none, perhaps, has served her with such unselfish devotion. Day and night, year in, year out, in storm and stress he had laboured incessantly, and ever his one thought had been for the honour of his country.

"He lay in his cabin, dying."

He had broken the power of Rupert, had wrested the dominion of the ocean from the Dutch, had humbled the power of Spain. He had sailed the Mediterranean as a conqueror, and had swept the narrow seas clear of England's foes. But, above and beyond all, he had lived a life so blameless that while his friends adored him, his very enemies could find nothing with which to reproach him.

Centuries have come and gone since that memorable day when the *St. George,* with her precious burden, sailed into Plymouth Sound; but the name of Blake still lives, and his example shines as a star for those who revere the memory of a true and valiant man.

COLLINS' CLEAR-TYPE PRESS.

Collins'

ILLUSTRATED POETS.

"The last word in Poets."

In Cloth, Gilt Top, **3/6**, and the following
Leather Bindings:

Long grain roan, limp, round corners, red under gold edges, gold roll.
Long grain roan, limp, round corners, red under gold edges, gold roll,
gilt fillet.
Seal Morocco, padded, round corners, red under gold edges, gold roll.
Crushed Morocco, padded, round corners, red under gold edges, gold roll.
Turkey Morocco, limp, round corners, solid red under gold edges, gold roll.
Turkey Morocco, padded, round corners, solid red under gold edges, gold roll.

This Popular Edition is bound in Ribbed Cloth, gold lettering on the
back, and *fac-simile* gold autograph on the side; gilt top.   Each Book
is set up from Collins' New Clear Type.

Each Book contains about 24 New Illustrations by Leading
Artists, some in colour.

1. Shakespeare.—Published, **4/-** With Biographical Introduction
   by Henry Glassford Bell.   Containing 65 Photo-Engravings.

2. Longfellow.—Complete Copyright Edition, by arrangement
   with Messrs. G. Routledge & Co., Ltd.; with Notes and
   Introduction by Walter Jerrold.   Illustrations by W. L. Taylor,
   G. C. Hindley, W. H. C. Groome, Paul Hardy, J. B. Greene, &c.

3. Wordsworth.—With Notes and Introduction by C. Kennett
   Burrow.   Illustrations by Harold Copping, C. J. Staniland,
   G. Grenville Manton, &c.

4. Milton.—With Notes and Introduction by Arthur Waugh.
   Illustrations by A. A. Dixon, J. Eyre, Herbert Cole, &c.

5. Burns.—With Notes and Introduction by Robert Ford.
   Illustrations by Walter G. Grieve, H. C. Preston Macgoun,
   Harold Copping, C. J. Staniland, &c.

6. Tennyson.—With Notes and Introduction by Arthur Waugh;
   containing 700 pages.   Illustrations by F. W. Hayes, P. Tarrant,
   Stanley Berkeley, K. Cameron, Herbert Cole, A. Banerle,
   J. Eyre, &c.

[Other Volumes in Preparation.]

Collins' Clear-Type Press.

New Illustrated Books for Boys and Girls.

New Volume of Adventure Stories.
COURAGE AND PERIL.
Containing 8 Coloured Plates and many Black and White Illustrations.

Cloth, Gilt Edges, 5/-; or Coloured Picture Boards, 3/-

This new volume contains exciting stories of adventure in all parts of the globe, and the numerous narratives of pluck and endurance and of strange happenings have the unusual merit of being true.

ALL ABOARD FOR STORYLAND.
Containing 8 Coloured Plates and many Black and White Illustrations by well-known Artists.

Cloth, Gilt Edges, 5/-; or Coloured Picture Boards, 3/-

The stories in this delightful book are from the pen of a practised writer for little folks, and are full of charm. The pictures, too, are of a very high quality, and letterpress and pictures alike will be found of the greatest attraction to our young people.

SWEET STORIES OF OLD.
Containing 8 Coloured Plates and many Black and White Illustrations.

Cloth, Gilt Edges, 5/-; or Coloured Picture Boards, 3/-

A delightful collection of favourite Bible Stories from the Old and New Testaments.

A FRIEND FOR LITTLE CHILDREN.
Coloured Picture Cover, Cloth Back, price 3/6.

A beautiful book of new Bible Pictures by the best artists of the day, no less than 32 full-page pictures—size, 12 × 10—appearing in the volume, together with a large number of new tinted engravings. The limited letterpress is printed in large type, and the reading is of a simple character for children.

CLAWS AND PAWS.
Coloured Picture Boards, price 2/6.
Pictures by Louis Wain, and Verses by Clifton Bingham.
A Series of Clever Studies of Cat and Dog Life.
14 Pages Coloured Illustrations, also Black and White Pictures.
Size, about 12½ × 10½ inches.

SUNDAY AFTERNOON STORIES.
Coloured Picture Boards, price 2/6.
16 Pages Coloured Illustrations, size, 12 × 10; also Black and White Pictures.

New Illustrated Books for Boys and Girls.

FROM FOREST, FIELD, AND FARM.
Containing 8 Coloured Plates and many Black and White Pictures.

4to, Cloth, Gilt Edges, 3/6; or Coloured Picture Boards, 2/-

Boys and Girls will hail with pleasure these quaint and attractive stories of life in forest and field, and they will learn a good many details of the habits of birds and animals. The pictures will prove an endless source of satisfaction, and the whole book will be eagerly welcomed.

FAIRY TALES FROM GRIMM.
Containing 8 Coloured Plates and many new Black and White Illustrations.

4to, Cloth, Gilt Edges, 3/6; or Coloured Picture Boards, 2/-

FAIRY TALES FROM HANS ANDERSEN.
Containing 8 Coloured Plates and many Black and White Illustrations.

4to, Cloth, Gilt Edges, 3/6; or Coloured Boards, 2/-

THE ADVENTURES OF ROBINSON CRUSOE.
With 48 Coloured Pictures and 32 Black and White Engravings.

4to, Cloth, 3/6.

THE PILGRIM'S PROGRESS AND HOLY WAR.
With 32 Coloured Pictures and many Black and White Engravings.

4to, Cloth, 3/6.

DARING AND DANGER.
WORLD WIDE ADVENTURES.
Each Book contains 4 Coloured and many Black and White Illustrations.

4to, Cloth, Gilt Edges, 2/6; or Coloured Picture Boards, 1/6.

SUNNY SMILES.
STORIES FOR SOMEBODY'S DARLINGS.
Each Book contains 4 Coloured and many Black and White Illustrations.

4to, Cloth, Gilt Edges, 2/6; or Coloured Boards, 1/6.

ANGELS ADORE HIM.
SUNDAY SUNBEAMS.
Each Book contains 4 Coloured and many Black and White Illustrations.

4to, Cloth, Gilt Edges, 2/6; or Coloured Picture Boards, 1/6.

Two new volumes of Bible Stories told in simple language for the little ones.

COLLINS' CLEAR-TYPE PRESS.

New Illustrated Books for Boys and Girls.

New One Shilling Picture Books.

Coloured Picture Boards. Demy Quarto.

THE STORKS and Other Tales from HANS ANDERSEN.

UNDER THE WILLOWS and Other Tales from HANS ANDERSEN.

THE WONDERFUL FIDDLER and Other Stories.

THE PRINCE WHO WAS NOT AFRAID. From GRIMM.

FEATHERS AND FUR.—Stories of Animal and Bird Life.

ANIMAL FRIENDS AND FOES.—New Stories and Pictures.

The attractive Picture Covers, the charming Illustrations, the pleasant Stories in simple language, the clear type, all tend to make this Series of exceptional merit, and represent the highest value for One Shilling.

One Shilling Each, Cloth.
Picture Boards, Ninepence.

NURSERY STORIES.	TALES OF ADVENTURE.
NURSERY SONGS.	FAVOURITE FAIRY TALES.
NURSERY TALES.	TRADITIONAL TALES.

This Series comprises a choice selection of Nursery Tales. Each Volume contains 8 Full-Coloured Pictures and Numerous Black and White Engravings.

New Painting Books.

GOLDEN TEXT PAINTING BOOK, 1/-
Scripture Texts, in Outline and Colour. 40 Pages. Size, 12 × 10.

HAPPY HOURS PAINTING BOOK, 1/-
Objects, Animals, and Flowers, in Outline and Colour. 46 Pages. Size, 12 × 10.

LITTLE TEXTS FOR LITTLE PAINTERS,
SUNDAY SUNSHINE PAINTING BOOK, 6d.
40 Pages. Size, 10 × 6.

LITTLE FOLKS PAINTING BOOK,
OUR DARLINGS PAINTING BOOK, 6d.
22 Pages. Size, 12 × 10.

Each Book has Full-Coloured Pictorial Cover, Varnished.

Children's Picture Toy Books.

Comprising an excellent collection of Nursery Stories and Rhymes, Fairy Tales, Humorous Verses, Stories of Animals, etc., etc., such as are calculated to delight little folks. Beautifully illustrated with Coloured Pictures and Black and White Engravings by Louis Wain, C. J. Staniland, Enoch Ward, J. Finnemore, A. A. Dixon, Harry Dixon, Harry Neilson, Miss Ellen Welby, and other well-known Artists.

The Designs on the Covers are most attractive, and are printed in bright, tasteful colours.

An important feature of these Picture Books is that they are entirely designed and printed in Great Britain.

Price Two Shillings.—Untearable.
Size, 12 × 10 inches. Printed on Thick Linen Paper.

RIDES WITHOUT HORSES.	NURSERY RHYMES.
ANIMAL PRANKS A B C.	COMIC CAPERS.
PUPPYLAND. By Louis Wain.	HAPPY DAYS AT THE FARM
THE A B C OF BIRDS.	BIBLE TREASURES.

Price One Shilling.—Untearable.
4to. Size, about 11 × 9 inches. Printed on Thick Cloth Lined Paper.
Strong Covers, Varnished, with Very Richly Coloured and Taking Designs.
Containing 8 Full-Coloured Pictures and 10 Pages Text and Engravings.

JACK AND THE BEAN-STALK.	THE WILD SWANS.
CINDERELLA.	THE TWO BROTHERS.
FAVOURITE NURSERY STORIES.	THE GOLDEN FLEECE.
DICK WHITTINGTON.	ALI BABA AND THE FORTY THIEVES.
PUNCH AND JUDY.	SEA BREEZES.
PUSS IN BOOTS.	PLAYTIME A B C.

Shilling Toy Books.
Large 4to. Size, about 12 × 10 inches.
Stiff Covers, Varnished, Cloth Back, Attractive Designs Printed in Colours on Paper.
Containing 16 Full-Coloured Pictures and 14 Pages Text.

RIDES WITHOUT HORSES.	STORIES AND PICTURES FROM THE BIBLE.
ANIMAL PRANKS A B C.	NURSERY RHYMES.
PUPPYLAND. By Louis Wain.	KITTENLAND.
THE A B C OF BIRDS.	SINDBAD, AND ALADDIN.
COMIC CAPERS.	ROBINSON CRUSOE (oblong 4to).
SOLDIERS, SHIPS, AND SAILORS.	HAPPY DAYS AT THE FARM (oblong 4to).
BIBLE TREASURES.	

COLLINS' CLEAR-TYPE PRESS.

4

Children's Picture Toy Books.

The Bold-Type Toy Books.—Sixpence.

4to. Size, about 11 × 9 inches.

Strong Covers, Varnished, Cloth Back, with Very Artistic Designs Printed in Colours.

PICTURES AND RHYMES.	CINDERELLA.
ALADDIN.	PUNCH AND JUDY.
FAVOURITE NURSERY STORIES.	PUSS IN BOOTS.
	SOLDIERS.
DICK WHITTINGTON AND HIS CAT.	SHIPS AND SAILORS.
	HEROES OF THE BIBLE.
JACK AND THE BEAN-STALK.	STORIES OF JESUS.

Untearable Sixpenny Toy Books.

Size, about 9½ × 7¼ inches.   Printed on Cloth Lined Paper.
Containing 6 Coloured Pictures, also Black and White Illustrations and Text.
Picture Covers Fully Coloured and Varnished.

PLAY AND PETS.	BILLS AND FEATHERS.
MY OWN ZOO.	LITTLE JACK HORNER NURSERY RHYMES.
FRIENDS IN FUR AND FEATHERS.	DICK WHITTINGTON AND HIS CAT.
PICTURES AND JINGLES.	
A B C OF RHYMES AND TOYS.	JACK AND THE BEAN-STALK.
FUNNY ANIMALS.	WILD ANIMAL STORIES.

The Stiff-Board Series.—Sixpence.

Size, about 10½ × 8 inches.
Coloured Pictorial Cover.   4 Coloured and many Black and White Pictures.

DOLLY DIMPLE.	PEACE ON EARTH.
OLD-TIME TALES.	THE RED SHOES.
FAIRY FAVOURITES.	THE MILLER'S DAUGHTER.
MY DOG ROVER.	I'LL TELL YOU A STORY.
THE SUNDAY STORY BOOK.	FLOSS AND HER FRIENDS.

New Threepenny Toy Books.

Size, about 9½ × 7¼ inches.   6 Coloured Illustrations and Black and White Pictures.

PLAY AND PETS.	BILLS AND FEATHERS.
MY OWN ZOO.	LITTLE JACK HORNER.
FRIENDS IN FEATHER AND FUR.	DICK WHITTINGTON.
PICTURES AND JINGLES.	JACK AND THE BEAN STALK.
A B C OF RHYMES.	
FUNNY ANIMALS.	WILD ANIMAL STORIES.

COLLINS' CLEAR-TYPE PRESS.

The "Young Pioneer" Series

Cloth, Gilt, - One Shilling.

Each containing Four Coloured Illustrations.

A Series of Entirely New Stories by the best known juvenile writers of the day, embracing Tales of adventure, travel, and general interest.

When the Ship Comes Home. By Jennie Chappell.

The Other One: A Story for Girls. By Miss Bedford

What Katy Did. By Susan Coolidge.

Jack Fraser's Adventures. By Herbert Hayens.

A Mystery of the Sea. By Herbert Hayens.

Will of the Mill. By G. Manville Fenn.

Audrey Marsh. By E. Everett-Green.

Young Peggy M'Queen. By Dr. Gordon Stables, R.N.

The Wurra Wurra Boys. By E. Harcourt Burrage.

Lost on the Saguenay. By Bessie Marchant.

In Days of Danger. By L. L. Weedon.

Manor Pool Island. By Harold Avery.

With the Rhodesian Horse. By Wm. Johnston.

Against the King. By Tom Bevan.

The Mysterious Head. By C. H. Hardisty.

"These attractive looking volumes . . . the names of the respective authors are a guarantee that the stories themselves are as full of adventure and excitement as they are pure and healthy in tone."—*Christmas Bookseller.*

"Issued at 1/- each, with four coloured illustrations, they are marvellous value."
—*St. James' Magazine.*

The "Forward" Series.

The Original Series, with Coloured Pictures.

New Attractive Bindings, in Art Colours.

Price, - - - **One Shilling.**

This Series of Books for Boys and Girls has been edited by Herbert Hayens, author of "Under the Lone Star," "A Fighter in Green," and numerous other Books for Boys; and care has been taken to publish only what can be confidently placed in the hands of youth.

Each Book is printed from Collins' Clear Type.

Andersen's Fairy Tales.

Grimms' Fairy Tales.

The Kopje Farm *(Copyright)*. By Wm. Johnston.

The Lost Jewel. By A. L. O. E.

The Captives of the Kaid *(Copyright)*. By Bessie Marchant.

The Quest of the Luck *(Copyright)*. By Lewis Ramsden.

The Lamplighter. By M. S. Cummins.

The Gorilla Hunters. By R. M. Ballantyne.

Home Sunshine. By C. D. Bell.

Two Years before the Mast. By R. H. Dana.

Good Wives. By L. M. Alcott.

Little Women. By L. M. Alcott.

Manco, the Peruvian Chief. By W. H. G. Kingston.

Masterman Ready. By Captain Marryat.

The Scalp-Hunters. By Captain Mayne Reid.

Tom Brown's School Days. By Thomas Hughes.

Feats on the Fiord. By Harriet Martineau.

Prince of the House of David. By Rev. J. H. Ingraham.

The Last of the Mohicans. By J. Fenimore Cooper.

Martin Rattler. By R. M. Ballantyne.

The Settlers in Canada. By Captain Marryat.

Danesbury House. By Mrs. Henry Wood.

The Rifle Rangers. By Captain Mayne Reid.

Peter the Whaler. By W. H. G. Kingston.

The Cruise of the Midge. By Michael Scott.

The Coral Island. By R. M. Ballantyne.

Additional Titles in Preparation.

COLLINS' CLEAR-TYPE PRESS.

Stories of Noble Lives.

Edited by HERBERT HAYENS.

Illustrated in Colour and Black and White.

In Handsome Cloth Bindings, Illustrated, - - 1/6.

To many boys and girls a pleasantly told biography is more attractive than even the most exciting work of fiction. "Peerless Women" contains sketches of large-hearted women, whose names are known throughout the Empire. "In the Icy North" tells in simple language the stories of Franklin and Nansen; while the "Two Old Sea Dogs" are Drake and Blake, beloved by our manly youth. "Missionary Pioneers"—the intensely interesting biographies of Moffat, Livingstone, Carey, Brainerd, and others. "Two Modern Travellers" are the lately deceased Mrs. Bishop and Sir Henry Stanley, whose stirring and adventurous careers will appeal very strongly to the youth of to-day.

Peerless Women. By Jeanie Douglas Cochrane.

In the Icy North: Franklin and Nansen. By Henry Harbour.

Two Old Sea Dogs: Drake and Blake. By Herbert Hayens.

Missionary Pioneers: Moffat, Livingstone, Carey, etc.
By Jeanie Douglas Cochrane.

Two Modern Travellers: Mrs. Bishop and Sir H. M. Stanley. By W. R. Richmond.

Others in Preparation.

Peerless Women.

By JEANIE DOUGLAS COCHRANE.

Crown 8vo, Illustrated, Cloth, - - - - - 1/6.

A series of word pictures of great women of the nineteenth century, admirably written and nicely illustrated in colour.

"The volume is one that should be read by all girls, for it is a record of splendid examples, of lives spent in noble endeavour, and the achieving of such success as does not spoil—as mere material success does sometimes—but illumines for ever the way of life for those who come after."—*Lady's Pictorial.*

"To single out any individual from this useful book would be making an invidious distinction. A perusal of all the 'lives' would act in an inspiring manner upon the mind of any girl worthy of her sex."—*Yorkshire Herald.*

"We can quite recommend it as a prize book."—*School Guardian.*

"A book that will be appreciated by girls of all ages."—*Manchester Courier.*

COLLINS' CLEAR-TYPE PRESS.

The "Challenge" Series.

Crown 8vo. Cloth. Size, $7\frac{1}{4} \times 4\frac{7}{8} \times 1\frac{1}{4}$ inches thick. With 8 Coloured Plates, 1/6.

Carefully selected and edited to provide sound, wholesome reading for Boys and Girls. Extremely suitable for Prize or Reward Books.

Mrs. Halliburton's Troubles. By Mrs. Henry Wood.

The Lamplighter. By M. S. Cummins.

Home Sunshine. By C. D. Bell.

The Gorilla Hunters. By R. M. Ballantyne.

Masterman Ready. By Captain Marryat.

The Prince of the House of David. By Rev. J. H. Ingraham.

The Channings. By Mrs. Henry Wood.

The Three Midshipmen. By W. H. G. Kingston.

The Wide, Wide World. By Elizabeth Wetherell.

The Pathfinder. By J. Fenimore Cooper.

Mistress Beatrice Cope. By M. E. Le Clerc.

The Coral Island. By R. M. Ballantyne.

The Settlers in Canada. By Captain Marryat.

Good Wives. By L. M. Alcott.

Little Women. By L. M. Alcott.

The Rifle Rangers. By Captain Mayne Reid.

Melbourne House. By Elizabeth Wetherell.

Martin Rattler. By R. M. Ballantyne.

Tom Brown's School Days. By Thomas Hughes.

The Last of the Mohicans. By J. Fenimore Cooper.

Danesbury House. By Mrs. Henry Wood.

Peter the Whaler. By W. H. G. Kingston.

Frank Fairlegh. By Frank E. Smedley.

Barriers Burned Away. By E. P. Roe.

John Halifax, Gentleman. By Mrs. Craik.

Additional Titles in Preparation.

Stories of Noble Lives.

In the Icy North:
The Story of FRANKLIN and NANSEN.

By HENRY HARBOUR,
Author of " Where Flies the Flag," etc., etc.

Crown 8vo, Illustrated, Cloth, - - - - - 1/6.

"Boys will enjoy this record of brave deeds."—*Sunday School Chronicle.*

"Boys with a taste for biography will be delighted."—*Great Thoughts.*

"Reads more like a story by Jules Verne than a true narrative of the dangers and hardships and perils experienced by the expeditions to the North Pole."—*Dublin Daily Express.*

"Most interesting and thrilling stories of adventurous heroism."—*Bristol Mercury.*

"Tells the wonderful story of Franklin and Nansen's Polar Discoveries."—*Record.*

Two Old Sea Dogs:
The Story of DRAKE and BLAKE.

By HERBERT HAYENS,
Author of " My Sword's My Fortune," " The President's Scouts," " For the Colours," etc., etc.

Crown 8vo, Illustrated, Cloth, - - - - - 1/6.

"A fine stirring, breezy, healthy story for boys. Once a boy gets his nose between its covers it will stay there to the word 'Finis.'"—*The Schoolmaster.*

"Brightly and vigorously written."—*Yorkshire Post.*

"Mr. Hayens' volume will have hosts of admirers."—*The Record.*

"The various incidents are described with a pen so graphic as to make the attraction to the reader even stronger than that of a novel."—*Dundee Courier.*

"Written in Mr. Hayens' most attractive style."—*Dublin Express.*

"This is a well-constructed tale, full of life and incident."—*Bristol Mercury.*

"Wonderful books at eighteenpence. These are precisely the sort of true stories that an intelligent gift-giver will put in the way of boys."—*Dundee Advertiser.*

"Just the thing for amusement as well as instruction."—*The Graphic.*

"Stories of the kind that will bear re-telling."—*Glasgow Herald.*

"A marvel of cheapness, tastefully bound and got up."—*Nottingham Express.*

"Are the best eighteenpenny books it has ever been our pleasure to read."
—*The Methodist Recorder.*

COLLINS' CLEAR-TYPE PRESS

The Graphic Story Books.

Eight Coloured Pictures.
Numerous Black and White Illustrations.
Cloth, Bevelled Boards, Olivine Edges, Price 2/-

An interesting series of Story Books for Young Readers, containing a number of entertaining tales and graphic descriptions of life and adventures in all parts of the world.

The matter is thoroughly healthy in tone, and has been written or carefully selected, so that Teachers and Parents may have no hesitation in placing any of these books in the hands of children under their charge.

As Prize books, and for School libraries, the series will be found very suitable, providing a large amount of good and interesting reading at a small cost.

Graphic Stories of Adventure
By Land and by Sea, at Home and Abroad.

Graphic Stories of Bravery
In many Lands, Afloat and Ashore.

Graphic Stories of Other Lands,
Describing Foreign Persons, Scenes, and Incidents.

Graphic Stories of Animals,
Tame and Wild, in all parts of the Globe.

Graphic Stories of Kings,
From Caractacus to Napoleon Bonaparte.

Graphic Stories of Soldiers
Whose exploits will never be forgotten.

Graphic Stories of the Sea,
Describing the Perils of the Deep.

Graphic Stories of Sailors
Who have braved great dangers and explored unknown regions.

Graphic Stories of Inventions
Which have benefited the Human Race.

Graphic Stories of Industries
Which give employment to millions of workers.

Graphic Stories from History,
In which Fact is stranger than Fiction.

Graphic Stories from Great Authors,
With a Sketch of their Lives.

COLLINS' CLEAR-TYPE PRESS.

The "Imperial" Library.

Large Crown 8vo. Size, 7½ × 5⅛ × 1½ inches. Bevelled Boards.

"Unequalled for Value."

Illustrated with **8 or 16** Coloured Illustrations.

The Three Midshipmen.   By W. H. G. Kingston.
The Swiss Family Robinson.   By W. H. G. Kingston.
Uncle Tom's Cabin.   By Mrs. H. B. Stowe.
Danesbury House.   By Mrs. Henry Wood.
The Last of the Mohicans.   By J. Fenimore Cooper.
The Pathfinder.   By J. Fenimore Cooper.
East Lynne.   By Mrs. Henry Wood.
Andersen's Fairy Tales.
Grimms' Fairy Tales.
The Wide, Wide World.   By Elizabeth Wetherell.
The Talisman.   By Sir Walter Scott.
The Channings.   By Mrs. Henry Wood.
Shirley.   By Charlotte Brontë.
Tom Brown's School Days.   By Thomas Hughes.
Two Years Ago.   By Charles Kingsley.
Pilgrim's Progress.   By John Bunyan.
Frank Fairlegh.   By Frank E. Smedley.
David Copperfield.   By Charles Dickens.
Little Women and Good Wives.   By L. M. Alcott.
Melbourne House.   By Elizabeth Wetherell.
Barriers Burned Away.   By E. P. Roe.
Westward Ho!   By Charles Kingsley.
Scottish Chiefs.   By Jane Porter.
Robinson Crusoe.   By Daniel Defoe.
John Halifax, Gentleman.   By Mrs. Craik.

Additional Titles in Preparation.

COLLINS' CLEAR-TYPE PRESS.

The "Herriot" Library.

In Handsome Ribbed Cloth, Gilt Top, Gilt Lettering, 2/-

Crown 8vo. Size, $7\frac{1}{4} \times 5$ inches.

The "Herriot" Library consists of Popular Works by Standard Authors. The volumes are clearly printed and handsomely bound. These volumes will add to the attractions of the book-buyers' shelves.

Each Book contains **Eight Black and White Illustrations** by the leading artists of the day.

The Channings.   By Mrs. Henry Wood.

The Prince of the House of David.   By the Rev. J. H. Ingraham.

The Scarlet Letter.   By Nathaniel Hawthorne.

The Pathfinder.   By J. Fenimore Cooper.

Masterman Ready.   By Captain Marryat.

The Cloister and the Hearth.   By Charles Reade.

The Woman in White.   By Wilkie Collins.

Great Expectations.   By Charles Dickens.

Jane Eyre.   By Charlotte Brontë.

It is Never too Late to Mend.   By Charles Reade.

The Mill on the Floss.   By George Eliot.

Danesbury House.   By Mrs. Henry Wood.

Burns' Poetical Works.   With Notes and Glossary.

East Lynne.   By Mrs. Henry Wood.

Tom Brown's School Days.   By Thomas Hughes.

Shirley.   By Charlotte Brontë.

Adam Bede.   By George Eliot.

Two Years Ago.   By Charles Kingsley.

Westward Ho !   By Charles Kingsley.

Kenilworth.   By Sir Walter Scott.

John Halifax, Gentleman.   By Mrs. Craik.

David Copperfield.   By Charles Dickens.

Milton's Poetical Works.

Tennyson's Poems.

Wordsworth's Poetical Works.

The "Herriot" Library.

Full Bound, Maroon Polished Leather, 5/-

Crown 8vo.   Size, $7\frac{1}{4} \times 5$ inches.

"A Handsome Economical Present."

The "Herriot" Library consists of Popular Works by Standard Authors. The volumes are clearly printed and handsomely bound. These volumes will add to the attractions of the book-buyers' shelves.

Each Book contains **Eight Black and White Illustrations** by the leading artists of the day.

The Channings.   By Mrs. Henry Wood.

The Prince of the House of David.   By the Rev. J. H. Ingraham.

The Scarlet Letter.   By Nathaniel Hawthorne.

The Pathfinder.   By J. Fenimore Cooper.

Masterman Ready.   By Captain Marryat.

The Cloister and the Hearth.   By Charles Reade.

The Woman in White.   By Wilkie Collins.

Great Expectations.   By Charles Dickens.

Jane Eyre.   By Charlotte Brontë.

It is Never too Late to Mend.   By Charles Reade.

The Mill on the Floss.   By George Eliot.

Danesbury House.   By Mrs. Henry Wood.

Burns' Poetical Works.   With Notes and Glossary.

East Lynne.   By Mrs. Henry Wood.

Tom Brown's School Days.   By Thomas Hughes.

Shirley.   By Charlotte Brontë.

Adam Bede.   By George Eliot.

Two Years Ago.   By Charles Kingsley.

Westward Ho!   By Charles Kingsley.

Kenilworth.   By Sir Walter Scott.

John Halifax, Gentleman.   By Mrs. Craik.

David Copperfield.   By Charles Dickens.

Milton's Poetical Works.

Tennyson's Poems

Wordsworth's Poetical Works.

The "Ideal" Library.

Cloth, Gold Lettering. Demy 8vo. **3/6.**

A Series of the Most Popular Books by Standard Authors.

Eight Coloured Pictures.

Grimms' Fairy Tales.

Andersen's Fairy Tales.

The Gorilla Hunters. By R. M. Ballantyne.

Mrs. Halliburton's Troubles. By Mrs. Henry Wood.

The Three Midshipmen. By W. H. G. Kingston.

Silas Marner. By George Eliot.

The Cloister and the Hearth. By Charles Reade.

The Channings. By Mrs. Henry Wood.

East Lynne. By Mrs. Henry Wood.

Stories of Adventure. **Fully Illustrated.**

Stories of the Sea and Sailors. **Fully Illustrated.**

Stories of Bravery. **Fully Illustrated.**

Masterman Ready. By Captain Marryat.

Tom Brown's School Days. By Thomas Hughes.

Shirley. By Charlotte Brontë.

Kenilworth. By Sir Walter Scott. **16 Pictures.**

Melbourne House. By Elizabeth Wetherell.

The Coral Island. By R. M. Ballantyne.

Robinson Crusoe. By Daniel Defoe. **16 Coloured Pictures.**

Pilgrim's Progress. By John Bunyan. **16 Coloured Pictures.**

Barriers Burned Away. By E. P. Roe.

Westward Ho! By Charles Kingsley.

John Halifax, Gentleman. By Mrs. Craik.

David Copperfield. By Charles Dickens. **16 Pictures.**

Adam Bede. By George Eliot.

Danesbury House. By Mrs. Henry Wood.

COLLINS' CLEAR-TYPE PRESS.

The "Ideal" Library.

New Edition.   New Cloth Binding.   Gold Lettering**.**

Demy 8vo.   Gilt Edges, 5/-

Each Book contains Eight Full-page Pictures.

A Series of the Most Popular Books by Standard Authors

Grimms' Fairy Tales.

Andersen's Fairy Tales.

The Gorilla Hunters.   By R. M. Ballantyne.

Mrs. Halliburton's Troubles.   By Mrs. Henry Wood.

The Three Midshipmen.   By W. H. G. Kingston.

Silas Marner.   By George Eliot.

The Cloister and the Hearth.   By Charles Reade.

The Channings.   By Mrs. Henry Wood.

East Lynne.   By Mrs. Henry Wood.

Stories of Bravery.   **Fully Illustrated.**

Masterman Ready.   By Captain Marryat.

Tom Brown's School Days.   By Thomas Hughes.

Melbourne House.   By Elizabeth Wetherell.

Barriers Burned Away.   By E. P. Roe.

David Copperfield.   By Charles Dickens.   **16 Pictures.**

Adam Bede.   By George Eliot.

Danesbury House.   By Mrs. Henry Wood.
